PRAISE FOR *WHAT*

In *What We Know For Sure*, Lia Ocampo and our colleagues from the U. S. Embassy in Manila, share their immigrant success stories. Each unique chapter leads us into their varied experiences. I am deeply honored that Lia requested that I write the "Praise For."

Foreign Service Nationals (FSNs) are critical to the success of every one of our embassies and consulates. U.S. law allows the most accomplished FSNs to immigrate with their spouses and single children (under the age of 21) to America. Lia's book is a first-person account of her own story and the stories of other former FSNs, many of whom I had the privilege to work with during my tenure as U.S. Ambassador from 2010 to 2013.

These co-workers and friends helped us weather numerous challenges including, assisting our military and the U.S. Agency for International Development save lives following devastating typhoons, respond to Chinese encroachment in the West Philippine Sea (South China Sea), educate at-risk children, combat human trafficking, assist indigent Americans, help those seeking to adopt babies, care for the over 300,000 American Veterans living in the Philippines, and provide safekeeping for over 17,000 heroes who paid the ultimate sacrifice during WW11 who are laid to rest at the Manila American Cemetery, our largest overseas burial ground.

These among other accomplishments too many to mention are why the FSNs in Manila were rewarded with the opportunity to immigrate to America. It is also why they have exceeded all expectations. They are well-educated, hardworking, religious, family-centered, and resilient. I confess to being biased regarding these irrepressible new Americans. I know them. I know their struggles.

I know their sacrifices. I know their heartbreaks. I know their longings for trips home, for prayers in their churches, for the smells of their favorite foods, for karaoke nights with friends, for the humid air of their birth land.
I know the pressure on them to send money and gifts home. Even with the resentment they face from some at home and the indignities from people in their new land about the vibrance of the Filipino culture, they choose to remain and strive in America.

It would be delightful if I could praise them for becoming as well-known and wealthy as other immigrants such as automaker Elon Musk or Filipino-Americans like White House Executive Chef Criseta Comerford and entrepreneur Dada Banatao. None have attained those lofty heights. Yet, each one of them are role models for future generations of FSNs, not only in Manila but for all our embassies. Daily they reaffirm the importance of immigrants to our nation's success.

Readers will find their stories informative and heart rendering. A testament to their individual and collective determination to build better lives in America for themselves and their families. They remind us of the importance of humility in starting over in a new land while at the same time demonstrating perseverance amid health scares, loss of family in the Philippines, and career challenges.

Mabuhay Lia and our colleagues. Salamat sa inyong lahat (thank you all) for your service to America and the Philippines.

HARRY K. THOMAS, JR.
(Ambassador Retired)

Inspirational Stories of Filipino Special Immigrants in America

What We Know For Sure

Volume One

by Lia

What We Know For Sure
Inspirational Stories of Filipino Special Immigrants in America

Digital Publishing of Florida, Inc.
Oldsmar, FL 34677

ISBN 978-1-949720-47-1

Printed in the United States
10 9 8 7 6 5 4 3 2

For more information or to contact the author, please go to www. AuthorLia.com

Inspirational Stories of Filipino Special Immigrants in America

What We Know For Sure

Volume One

To my mother,

Mercedes Papasin,
who taught me the value of reading,
skills in typing, proofreading,
and how to speak Spanish.

To my children,

Jonathan, Mary Frances, and Joshua,
who are often my supporters, and critics.

FOREWORD

Walk by faith and not by sight. Write your own story. Follow your dreams.

Lia Ocampo shared with me these words to live by as we continued to talk about the many other inspiring lines written as watermarks on her "vision board" in her tiny Florida apartment.

Twenty-five years ago, I had the opportunity to shake hands with Lia when I processed my human resources documents as a new employee of the American Embassy Manila. I was waiting in the HR waiting area when Lia passed by and asked me if I was being helped by someone. She was then working as one of the two locally employed staff assigned to handle HR management of American employees. Her cheerful demeanor and kind spirit sent positive vibes in the room. I knew then that Lia would be that kind of friend you would have for life. Fast forward, Lia left HR and moved to the sister agency of the trade department where I was assigned. In those times, we had many deep conversations about life, family, friendships, and the daily commute around Metro Manila.

When her former agency decided to close the program in Manila, Lia quickly transitioned from one U.S. Government agency to another, serving a full cycle of human resource management experience. We've kept in touch, despite her new assignments, until she capped her HR career at the embassy in 2012. Then she moved to America under the special immigrant visa program.

In 2015, I had the opportunity to see Lia again in Denver when I visited for a work training. It was our very first reunion after her immigration. She gave me that real precious day in between her flight assignments and I'm personally grateful for her generosity of time. In  2019, Lia made a stop in New Orleans en route to her next flight schedule to again meet with me while I was visiting for another work conference. I couldn't fathom that she again took time to see me and I would always be grateful for her kindness.

We found ourselves in a very engaging conversation about how she can champion the idea of coming up with a book project beyond her travel snippets and blogs. While she has written hundreds of stories about her personal experience, world travels, and the journey she blazed while living in America, it wasn't easy to see that project through to fruition. Lia had to contend with managing personal resources to pull together the book project while also juggling work schedules and shuttling between Florida and New York to attend to her youngest son.

For more than 25 years now, Lia and I shared many life stories. We had the common ground of serving the United States Embassy Filipino Employees Association, our personal advocacy to promote literacy and leadership development among the youth, and same passion for books and travel. We are taking the same pathway with a stronger resolve to enjoy womanhood in our golden years and live a more meaningful life in general.

Lia's passion to go beyond one's comfort zone and taking the risks is truly inspiring and worthy of emulation. When we share personal stories and breakthroughs, they can help create a bridge for another person to cross. Lia created that bridge in her vision book project when she encouraged her peers and former work colleagues to share their personal breakthroughs as immigrants in America. Lia's indefatigable character built a strong personal foundation in order to live a meaningful life and become an inspiration for others.

With this book, Lia found what she calls her "life's purpose," which is to be a positive influence and a life coach, someone who helps other people find their own personal success.

Lia chooses to see the glass half full rather than half empty. And she chose to make the next generation of aspiring individuals to benefit from her great work. Her desire to help and take the extra mile to guide future immigrants is not only a deep manifestation of her commitment to serve but also the true epitome of a selfless and fearless leader ready to transcend boundaries and fulfill infinite possibilities.

Thess Sula
February 3, 2020
Manila, Philippines

PREFACE

Everyone has a story to tell. And in everyone's story there is value. How good would it be if we could sit around and share our lives, our truths, our experiences, and our knowledge with others? Would you share what you've learned in your life if you knew it might help someone else?

It is this very premise that inspired me to write this book. As a child born, raised, and educated in the Philippines, I went to work for the United States Embassy and fulfilled my dream to come to America. My focus was to make a better life for my children. That journey has given me a mountain of stories to share. Stories that I hope will help potential immigrants and other immigrants so they can learn, grow, or find comfort in a shared experience.

What We Know for Sure was initially inspired by my recently completed mission I called "Mission Africa." A mission designed to help five young girls in Africa learn how to set and achieve their goals. My next mission was called "Mission Philippines." The objective of this mission was to speak with my former colleagues from the U.S. Embassy and learn their stories. I then shared them in this book so others could benefit.

Countless immigrant stories in America have been told and retold. You see them on television, hear them from other people, or witness them with your own eyes. Some of these immigrants are making history as leaders and advocates for others. But most of them are ordinary people with dreams to fulfill and goals to achieve. This book features former embassy employees who provided long, faithful, and valuable service to the United States Government. Their stories are both unique and inspiring. These individuals are equipped with many assets. They are trained and skilled in the process of immigration. In this book, they share the process of coming to America and the truth behind the hard work and sacrifices it takes to stay.

What We Know for Sure was written for potential immigrants and immigrants, no matter what stage of the process they are in. These stories are here to comfort, inspire, educate, and guide any immigrant throughout his or her journey to the land of the free.

INTRODUCTION

Are you ready? Are you prepared for the work and sacrifice involved in immigrating to the United States? Is your family ready? Immigration is a huge undertaking, but it is done all the time, and I am here to share my story and the stories of many other immigrants to help and inspire you through the process.

Acquiring the Special Immigrant Visa (SIV) was the biggest privilege I got from working for the American government–my salary, training, and experiences were all secondary. I knew if I dedicated myself, my time, my service, my talents, and my skills that the chance to apply for the SIV would come. And after 18 years, I sat looking at my binder full of accomplishments, awards, training certificates, and other correspondence. My papers more than proved I had the necessary exemplary service requirements ready to gain my SIV two years prior to the normal 20 years required. This early exemption was critical for my children who were quickly coming to the age when they would no longer be able to immigrate with me. So, when the decision was made and I was approved to receive my SIV, I was both excited and eager to begin the process.

The American Embassy was a big part of my life and the others who shared their stories in this book. When it came time to apply, some of us were unsure about it but for different reasons. Some have older kids they had to leave behind, others didn't want to start all over, and some had no choice but to stay for familial reasons. But for those of us that made the decision to leave, we could only plan and hope that things would be ok.

Once each of us made the fateful decision to apply for a visa, the floodgate opened, and questions poured in: Which state do I settle in? With whom will my family and I stay? What will my job be? Will I buy or rent a home? How much money will I bring? Will I sell my properties in the Philippines or do I rent them out? Should I leave my kids behind to finish school? These questions are just the tip of the iceberg of decisions when applying for the SIV.

Although several of us from the embassy took this path together, we each had very different family situations. Some had the advantage of asking for information, guidance, and support from friends or family already living in the United States. And some had no one waiting for them and sought advice from our colleagues who did.

As much as each of us carefully planned our paths, not everything went as planned. There were last minute changes before leaving, situations altered upon arrival, and even more unexpected challenges weeks after we got here. We had to be prepared for the unexpected and learn to make the tough decisions whether we wanted to or not.

Eventually, we each settled and acquired all the appropriate documentation: social security numbers, permanent resident cards, state identification cards, driver's licenses, bank accounts, and credit cards. Then we enrolled our kids into schools and found jobs. We could finally breathe, right? The truth was that was when the real work began and why I wrote this book.

We all started from humble beginnings. Our transition from the Philippines to the American lifestyle and workforce was no piece of cake. We went through hard times and made mistakes but in the end, we learned and grew. These stories are real. They happened to real people and I am excited to share them with you. Let these stories prepare you, guide you, inspire you, and provide comfort on your path to finding success and happiness in America.

CONTENTS

"Everywhere immigrants have enriched and strengthened the fabric of American life."

- *John F. Kennedy*

1

LIA OCAMPO

Human Resources Specialist
Human Resources Office
U.S. Department of Veterans Affairs
18 years of service

I begin my story with a favorite song:
"Oh New York, New York.
If I can make it here, I can make it anywhere,
that's what they say.
I'm gonna make it by any means,
I got a pocket full of dreams."

My vision had always been to create a bright future, inspire others, and make a positive impact on the world. Born and raised in the Philippines, I witnessed poverty and fewer opportunities. And while many accepted this path, I dreamed of a better life for me and my children. I desired

greater opportunities for careers, housing, transportation, medical care, health insurance, and overall lifestyle. But I also understood that immigrating to America would take time, hardwork, faith, and determination to face the challenges and difficult choices that would come my way. I was more than ready.

My journey to America started long before I immigrated. And during that time, I learned to use my two great passions–journalism and photography–to create a voice for myself and for others. I became an advocate for women's rights, social responsibility, and volunteerism. My eyes and ears were always searching for those positive voices and stories to capture and retell to motivate and inspire those around me.

This book is the result of what I saw and heard during the many years in the Philippines as I prepared to immigrate and the years since I came to America. It is a compilation of stories from myself and others who came to the United States and the lessons we learned along the way. My mission is to give hope, comfort, and support for future immigrant families as they face the challenges of immigrating.

***

My children and I moved swiftly through the terminal so I could make it to my gate on time. The night before I hadn't slept at all as I had a long list of things to do before I left. But by the time we made it to the airport, all I felt was excitement.

"I won't be here, but you know what I expect?" I asked, looking at all three of my children as they stood before me.

All three of them nodded yes.

"Be good and study well. We will all be together soon." We hugged tightly, and I gave each one a final good-bye kiss and then headed to my gate. The prior two months had been a whirlwind of activity. I received my approval for my Special Immigrant Visa in May, and I was boarding the plane in July. Tired both emotionally and physically, I needed the rest that the plane ride would give me. I remember being thankful for the exhaustion as I knew sleep would get me through the long flight ahead.

I arrived in the "Big Apple" in July of 2012, carrying two suitcases packed with my necessities: framed pictures of my children, my resume, my favorite clothes, and what I hoped would be enough money to get me through. My decision to leave the Philippines was in some ways very easy, but in other ways challenged me to my core. I had spent 18 years working for the United States Embassy all for the chance to immigrate with the goal of bringing my children with me. Although you needed 20 years as an employee to be eligible for the Special Immigrant Visa (SIV), my years of exemplary service to the embassy allowed me to receive an exemption and I was granted my SIV after 18 years.

My two eldest children, Jonathan and Mary Frances, were 20 and 19 respectively and were far into their college education. And despite them being included on my petition for my SIV, I feared moving them to America. The adjustment would be too difficult for them. If they stayed and finished college and began their careers in the Philippines, their transition to the States, when the time came, would be much more seamless. They would gain not only their education but valuable work experience to apply to a job here in the States.

My youngest child, Joshua, was only 11 in 2012. And though it pained my heart both physically and emotionally to leave him behind, I knew he needed to stay as well. Since he was a baby he was looked after by his nanny and she would continue to do so after I left. Taking him from his friends, the only home he ever knew, leaving his siblings behind, and moving to a new country would have been too much for him. The hurt I felt for leaving was only made better by knowing that the situation was temporary. My children had each other to lean on, with their dad, in my absence.

Many times, throughout the years, people asked me why I chose New York of all the places to live. My answer would always be that I had intended to work for the United Nations. I had even created an online profile, continually scanned their site for job openings, and applied multiple times. But it was not meant to be, despite there being one close call where I almost got hired. My mind wouldn't let me accept this setback as a failure. Instead I saw it as a blessing, and a push in the direction I was meant to be in–although I had no idea what that was right away.

From the moment the plane landed on U.S. soil, I had set myself for acclimatization. I made the choice to delay finding a job so that I could travel, learn the culture, make some connections, and establish a home base for myself before hitting the job market. I called this time "my vacation." I wasn't on a beach or at a resort sipping a cocktail with an umbrella in it, but I was free from the confines of a job and devoted to absorbing as much of my new home as possible.

One of my favorite trips I took was to Boston. On my birthday, I went to visit the famed Harvard University. As I stood in front of its majestic entrance, I felt an overwhelming sense of accomplishment; a major part of my life's dream had been realized. I continued to take in the sights by the water and couldn't believe the number of places to eat in Haymarket Square. I had landed in the middle of voluminous possibilities and I promised myself not to waste the opportunities I had worked so hard for.

The first place I called home was a dark basement apartment. There were steep, narrow stairs that led to a door. Once inside you walked right into the kitchen. There were no windows to allow natural light. I had one tiny room that just had enough space for a single bed and my things. I shared the one bathroom and the kitchen with several other tenants. I had grown up in a similar environment, so perhaps that is why I didn't mind the place initially. I could handle it until I couldn't. The noise bothered me. In the mornings when I tried to sleep, people were outside my bedroom door talking. I had no privacy. So, after two months I found another place. The new place wasn't much different than the first and within three months I was moving again. I missed the quiet and peacefulness of the condo I left in the Philippines. And surprisingly I missed driving. There is something about driving yourself where you want to go and not being dependent on a subway to take you there. But, like adapting to living with strangers in a small, crowded, noisy apartment, I had to learn to live with taking the subway whenever I needed to. The homeless in the subway stations in the early morning, or the thick, foul stench that ruled the air as you waited for your train to move, were just some of the costs of achieving my goals.

Every week I had set aside time to talk with my kids. And no matter where I was living, the first thing I did was unpack their photos and place them next to my bed. Their faces were the last thing I saw at night and the first thing I saw in the morning. Keeping them close and talking when we could got me through those difficult and lonely times. I would tell myself, time and time again, *you chose this Lia, so you can't be sad or unhappy. You will achieve your dream.*

When I started looking for work, my search became a full-time job. I kept a steno-pad filled with lists. I wrote down every company and position I applied for to track my progress. I went on every interview that I got. I took nothing for granted. Overtime, I gained so much interview practice that my nerves finally calmed, and I found the confidence I needed when I talked to potential employers.

Although I had planned my money out carefully before leaving the Philippines, accounting for the time I would be unemployed, I still found myself with less funds than I needed. New York was expensive and with no money coming in, reality hit hard. I soon found I had almost no funds. I sought solace with my two friends Marichu and Hazel. Marichu and I had been best friends since college, and I knew if I reached out to her she would help me. Marichu understood my dilemma and wired me money immediately. A short time after, I realized I wouldn't have enough money for my rent. So, this time I texted my friend Hazel in Arizona. Hazel and I are close friends and we had met while working at the embassy. She empathized with my struggles and sent me money right away. Their understanding and generosity helped me through those initial months in the States before I found employment. I cried for their generosity and for the humbling fact that I needed this help more than I let myself realize. I will be forever grateful for their willingness to help and their friendship.

In what seemed like my never-ending job search, I joined one of the many organizations available to immigrants. This organization helps recent immigrants apply their skills, education, and previous experiences to the U.S. workforce. I happened to discover them on the internet one day and immediately applied for their program. I got accepted. They taught me advanced job search skills and I honed my interviewing skills through their mock interviews.

In addition to joining an organization designed to help immigrants, I read about a program at Pace University to receive a Human Resources Generalist certificate. I knew the more I could put on my resume in terms of experience, education, and certifications, the better chance I had to land a job. But this course was not cheap. I didn't let that stop me. I emailed the campus registrar and told them my story. Thankfully they granted me a discount, and I was on my way to getting the additional certification.

My interviewing skills ramped up and my new certification added to my resume, I got my first job. Eight months after my plane had touched down on U.S. soil, I had a place to live, had done some travel, and I was employed by a large non-profit organization as a recruiter. As a recruiter, I was tasked with finding clients a job while they received government assistance. Even though the job was temporary, I felt blessed to have started my new life and finally have some money coming in. Eventually after that job ended, I went to work temporarily for Macy's department store as a personal shopper. Though the job was short-lived, I gained a new customer service skill to take with me. Every experience became a hotbed of knowledge I could add to my resume. Each new job, no matter how long it lasted, was a chance to be better than I was before, and I was eternally grateful.

Hard work is just part of who I am. My mother raised me to value education and to work hard. I was staying true to my roots as I acclimated to my new life, even without my kids or the comforts I left behind. Some days were difficult, but mostly I found comfort in meeting others and pushing myself to do better. Living for my future here with my kids was always the goal.

In the beginning of 2014, I was recommended to work for a Korean pop entertainment company. I knew nothing about the Korean pop scene or anything about the Korean culture. Back in the Philippines I had worked as a citizen journalist for CNN iReport. Writing and photography were always my passions. So, when the Korean pop job required me to hire writers and edit their work, I was more than interested. I accepted the position and began training for the job.

By the second week in, I knew I had made a mistake. Editing work of writers meant I was in a cubical, staring at a computer all day, and trying to edit something I knew nothing about. Isolated and more out of my element than I had ever been since immigrating, I knew I had to leave. The boss got wind of my unhappiness and came over pleading, "No, don't go please. Give it some more time and you'll love it here." As always, I listened to that inner voice which screamed for me to leave. When I walked out of the building that day, and as I stood on the sidewalk, I looked up at the sky, and thought, *You came here to find happiness, you came here to grow and make a life for your kids when they come over, don't settle now. You'll find the job that's right for you, faith will guide you.*

Someone once asked if I was fearful making that decision, "Weren't you worried about how you would pay your bills?"

"No. I'm fearless, I guess. I knew something else would come along. And I also knew that I made incredible sacrifices to achieve my dreams, that settling for less than what made me happy was on par with giving up. I would never give up."

My faith didn't fail me. Soon after my resignation an employment agency picked me up and I was back to work as a customer service representative for New York City Department of Consumer Affairs. And although this was miles better than working for the Korean company, I needed more. I guess wanting more has been my driver all along. I thought about my mother and all her advice. I knew one day I would have the life I desired. That's when I had relaxed enough in my new life to let myself think about an old dream. During my college years, I had aspired to become a flight attendant. My innate love of adventure and travel made that dream lock in my brain, but it had been put away on hold for years. So, one day after coming home and flopping on my tiny bed from exhaustion, I remembered that young woman and the dream she had. My tenacity showed through again, as I challenged myself to fulfill that dream no matter what it took.

A regional carrier accepted my application and I headed to training school. The training time was intense, as we were taught at warp speed and tested every other day. I struggled to keep up, but I was optimistic, just as I was about so many things in life. If a person failed to pass the required exams they risked being dropped from the class. I was still there when it came time for the final exam, so I pushed myself to the limit to pack in all the information I needed to know. I would wake up very early and go into the bathroom to study so I wouldn't bother my roommate.

I took the final exam but worried that I hadn't passed. I wasn't a super detailed person and I learned differently than the other students. But when the scores were handed out and I saw mine, I broke down. My tears flowed like a river, leaving my eyes puffy and red. For the first time in a very long time I let my emotions pour out of me with no attempt to control them. I had done it. I had achieved another dream of mine.

I called my friends ecstatic with the news, "You are doing what?" they asked.

"I am a flight attendant! Can you believe it?"

"You can't swim! Didn't you have to pass some swimming exam?"

"Nope. They didn't require it. And I passed everything else, so I am on my way!"

We all laughed. I knew they were happy for me. I was happy for me. Excited to start my dream job while living in the country I wanted to and all that was left to make it perfect was for my kids to join me.

My story is like so many other immigrants' but for all their similarities, we can learn something new from each other's stories. It's why I have assembled 25 stories from friends and colleagues who have made the journey to America and compiled the lessons they learned, so that along with my story, you can also gain from their wisdom.

2

FE SACRO

Legal Instrument Examiner
Fiduciary Unit, Field Section, U.S. Department of Veterans Affairs
32 years of service

Leaving a long-time career and comfortable life isn't easy. But change can be good, especially if it concerns the future of our children. To give the best for them is what we do as parents. Fe is truly admirable for giving up a lot in exchange for her daughter's better or yet best life.

I took the plunge and pursued the "American Dream." My daughter is the ultimate reason I applied for SIV to give her better career options, more benefits, and an array of experience. I immigrated in 2013 with my husband, before my daughter turned 21 to ensure she got her permanent resident status.

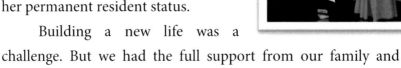

Building a new life was a challenge. But we had the full support from our family and friends. Slowly, we started to adapt to the new culture and lifestyle. We built our credit, acquired the needed transportation, successfully went through the tedious apartment selection, and finally moved into our new home. Meanwhile, our daughter built her career experience.

We gave our daughter not just an option but the decision to have a better future. Now she enjoys a great job with the County of Santa Clara in California.

I miss my long-time career serving Veterans and their families and the camaraderie in Veterans Affairs. It was a tough decision to leave the life we had, but it was a great change.

Courage and resilience have been my family's investment over the past few years. I'm thankful to achieve my goal for my daughter. I continue to be optimistic that more blessings are coming our way, with persistence and faith.

Your future accomplishments as well as that of your children are ahead of you. Make the decision. Take the plunge and persevere.

3

VIC SAN JUAN

Agent Cashier
Financial Management Center
27 years of service

DINAH SAN JUAN

Decision Review Officer
U.S. Department of Veterans Affairs
29 years of service

Education is one of the best legacies we can provide our children. It helps them seize great opportunities that lead to a greater achievement. Vic and Dinah gave their daughters good education. They have an inspiring story of love and sacrifice.

B eing apart for four years was a great sacrifice. For our daughters' sake, we had to do it.

We never imagined we would leave the Philippines someday and live in America. Our life was comfortable back home. Our main reason for leaving our jobs with the embassy was for the future of our daughters. We took advantage of this wonderful privilege before our older daughter turned twenty-one.

We had a family meeting because it involved a big change for all of us. Initially, our daughters were against the idea of leaving their friends behind. They didn't understand why we had to uproot them from the lifestyle they enjoyed.

Vic and I decided to do it despite our daughters' objections. We knew it would be hard to start all over again. Our older daughter was on her fourth year in college and our younger daughter had three more years to finish. We didn't want to leave anyone behind, so we had to strategize.

Vic and our daughters immigrated in 2008. Our SIV application says that I was "to follow." It means I had to file another application when it's time for me to leave.

We were aware that college education in the U.S. is expensive, and we wouldn't likely be able to afford the cost. This was our strategy: Vic was left behind in the U.S. to find a job while me and the girls went back to the Philippines to finish their college education. We  applied for a reentry permit for our younger daughter to maintain her permanent resident status. Meanwhile, I continued to work at the embassy to provide a steady income for our family while Vic was looking for a job.

Vic's life wasn't easy, but he was willing to try anything. He spent a long 12 hours each day looking for job opportunities. Fortunately, his cashier experience came in handy when he was hired at a local bank.

Our older daughter finished her medical technology degree. After passing the Philippine board exam, she flew back to the U.S. to join her dad. The two of them lived in a small studio apartment. It was a hard situation; she felt alone while her dad was working. She cried almost every day and begged him to send her back. The changes in the weather, especially during winter, made her situation worse.

After a year, we obliged. She went back to the Philippines to prepare for the U.S. board exam at a review center. She went back to the U.S. after the review, took her U.S. certification, and passed. She started job hunting and was hired at Georgetown University Hospital. Her mindset started to change. She skyped me when she received her first paycheck and was excited to tell me, "This is equivalent to a one-year salary of my counterpart in the Philippines." She finally realized why we had to uproot them and sacrifice our comfortable life in the Philippines.

It was difficult for Vic to start a new life in America. But it was more challenging for me to carry on by myself and do the things he used to do like changing a flat tire, being stranded alone in the flooded streets of Metro Manila, and getting home 4-5 hours later.

We're able to achieve our goal for our daughters to finish their studies in the Philippines. Our younger daughter graduated with a degree in physical therapy and passed her Philippine board exam. Subsequently, we left the Philippines for good. We are thankful that after four long years of being separated, our family is whole again. Modern technology made our temporary separation bearable.

My twenty-nine years of working for the U.S. Department of Veterans Affairs in the Philippines was a rewarding career. My heart still belongs to the Veterans. I now work for the State Veterans Service Organization and continue to serve them. Our daughters are both married, and they have great careers in the medical field. And our lives are easier again being together.

To move from one part of the world to another wasn't an easy feat. It took courage and lots of prayers. With the help of our families and friends, we were able to rise above all the trials. There will be more challenges in the future, but such is life.

For the San Juans – it was all worth it.

4

ARNEL CARAS

Operations Supervisor
Social Security Administration
29 years of service

JULIET CARAS

Cashier
U. S. Department of Veterans Affairs
25 years of service

Wisdom is not just a state of being wise. It's the ability to try, analyze, reflect, and learn from experiences. When you apply this wisdom to make your life better, you become wise. Arnel and Juliet have much wisdom to share. They've been tested, yet their faith grew bigger and their love stronger.

"**I** was hungry, and you gave me food. I was thirsty, and you gave me a drink. I was a stranger, and you welcomed me." Matthew 24:35. This favorite Bible verse from the book of Matthew has guided us in our lives in America.

If it had been just for me and Juliet, we would not have immigrated. Our life in the Philippines was blessed both spiritually and financially. We were surrounded with supportive families and friends. We had a solid foundation of our spiritual lives.

The time came when we had to decide whether or not to pursue the SIV. We had five children ages 20, 19, 18, 17, and 6. The future of our children was the main reason why we're here.

Before we decided, we sought the guidance of a priest. His message to us was clear. To move or seek other places for greener pastures is normal. But material gain shouldn't be the priority. Spiritual matter is most important.

It was hard to leave our religious community called "Pag-ibig (Love) for God Catholic Community." We were active in the Youth Ministry since 1991. We missed doing community service for the less privileged and people in need. We loved our "Bible study." Our children were also involved by attending the Bible studies, monthly assemblies, and other activities. It was one of the best things that happened to our family.

We immigrated in 2006 to Jacksonville Florida. Relatives welcomed us, and we stayed in their home for three months until we found a place of our own.

Longing to be able to continue our spiritual journey, we joined a religious organization called "Couples For Christ."

Household meetings and assemblies were held monthly. "Seek first the kingdom of God and everything shall be added unto you."

To be able to continue my federal employment was my main goal. I was fortunate to get my first job as a disability specialist at the Florida Department of Health. After eight years working for the State, I resigned to pursue my goal to continue my career with the Social Security Administration. We moved to Washington State when a position was offered to me. It was my steppingstone to gain entry to federal service. But not for long; a new job opportunity opened in Central Florida, so we moved back. I retired in 2019.

Juliet, on the other hand, started her career as a teller at a local bank; it lasted for six years. She's also now retired after working as a finance representative for three years at a hospital.

Looking back, I believe we made the right decision to pursue the SIV. Our children are now successful in their chosen careers. We now have three beautiful grandchildren who give us so much joy and pride.

As new "retirees," we now have more time to enjoy our grandchildren. We also have more time to share the blessings God has graced upon us.

"Truly I say to you, as you did it to one of the least of my brethren, you did it to me." Matthew 24:50

We were once strangers in America. Opening the door of our home to our colleagues and friends who needed a temporary shelter to stay was a joyful and rewarding experience. You can do it, too.

"How much better to get wisdom than gold, to get insight rather than silver." Proverbs 16:16

Humans continue to seek a better life. We continue to accumulate material gain. We have goals and dreams to fulfill. However, these are achievements we can only possess in our lifetime here on earth.

Seek wisdom from people who've walked further down the path than you. We're here to share this wisdom through this book. And seek wisdom in the Word of God.

"Trust in the Lord with all your heart and lean not on your own understanding; in all your ways, submit to Him and He will make your paths straight." Proverbs 3:5-6

Our journey wasn't straight and smooth. But we sought guidance and drew strength from God. He led us to the path where we were supposed to go.

"Have I not commanded you? Be strong and courageous. Do not be afraid; do not be discouraged, for the Lord your God will be with you wherever you go." Joshua 1:9

Wherever we go, remember - there's a better home where we are welcomed, and a better goal to see our loving family in heaven.

TO GOD BE THE GLORY!

5

RUDY LIMLINGAN

Budget Supervisor
Financial Management Center
28 years of service

BELINDA LIMLINGAN

Public Affairs Program Assistant
Public Affairs Office
23 years of service

Survival means existence. And existence means purpose. Giving the best for our children is the reason why we exist as parents. Bing and Rudy have experienced the real meaning of survival and defeat. That experience has taught them a hard lesson. It was their turning point in deciding that their sons deserved a better life. They provided them with opportunities, tools, and resources to explore their dreams, and survive.

S ome people asked us, "Do we really need to leave our comfort zone and start all over from rock bottom to achieve the elusive American dream? Are you certain that it would be for the benefit of your children? Are you ready to humble yourself and eat your pride? Is it worth leaving your aging parents?"

These were some questions thrown at us when we were considering immigrating to America.

We met at the embassy and got married in 1993. Together, we built our service and our family with high hopes to give our children a good education and a better future.

We were blessed with two boys, and one of them needed extra care and training due to his learning disabilities. We've tried to get him into good schools and spent quite a sum to address his special needs. But our special education system in the Philippines wasn't ready to adapt a sustainable program to help people with disabilities.

Our other son has a promising future ahead of him and was getting ready to grow his wings and fly. We wanted him to be successful and get a stable source of income so he could help his brother when our time has come to end.

Fast forward to 2012, we lost a brother-in-law and a brother in a span of almost a month. They were two contrasting cases but ended similarly: death at an early age due to lack of proper medical facilities and treatment. This made us realize

that it wasn't enough to give our children a good education. We needed to make sure that we could give them a better chance of survival to realize and explore their best dreams.

It's never easy to uproot your family and start all over in a foreign country with limited family support. But we didn't want our children blaming us when we're old and gray that they could have done better if only we had brought them to America. At least, in doing so, we left no stone unturned and we wanted to help motivate our colleagues who might consider the same path.

With all these plans, we always sought guidance and prayed even harder to Our Lord. Strong faith and devotion through prayers will always pave ways to great prospects and will never fail you.

Through this sharing, we give helpful advice that might work for you, but it's never etched in stone, so nothing is concrete and fool proof.

First piece of advice: Reconnect with friends and former colleagues to find the best place where your expertise will be in demand.

Our initial plan was for Bing to bring our eldest, Daniel, to America, leaving Rudy and Dave in the Philippines while we tried to get settled and find the best state to start growing our roots. After securing our visas, we reconnected with some of our former supervisors and colleagues and asked them what were the possible states where we could find jobs.

Ms. Vivian Lesh, former financial management officer, informed us that the Post Support Unit in Charleston, South Carolina was looking for a budget analyst. Rudy was a good candidate, as they were hiring first time immigrants familiar with the government accounting system and procedures.

❖ LESSONS LEARNED
  ➢ It won't hurt to ask around about possible job opportunities.
  ➢ Stay in touch with friends and former colleagues.

Second piece of advice: Get ready to grab the first opportunity.

Rudy applied for the budget analyst position, gave his best shot, and was hired. We changed our initial plans; he joined our party of two. He submitted his documents and worked on his clearance. We made our entry to America in February 2015.

Rudy received his social security number, flew back to the Philippines and filed his resignation. Daniel and I stayed in Pennsylvania for few months looking for a job with limited travel.

❖ LESSONS LEARNED
  ➢ Pray harder and keep your focus.
  ➢ Grab all the opportunities that come along your way.
  ➢ Always keep your options open.

Which comes first, chicken or egg?

Reliable transportation was our first chicken or egg situation. The question about access to reliable transportation came when we started applying for a job.

We were rescued by a former colleague and true friend, Kelly. She opened her home to Daniel and me while we tried to figure out what we should do first. She let Daniel use her car to take the practical driving test. He passed the test without issues.

- ❖ LESSONS LEARNED
  - ➤ If you're not a skilled driver, take driving lessons.
  - ➤ Practice your driving skills and consciously follow all traffic rules.
  - ➤ Drive as far as you could to build that confidence and the experience of hardcore driving.
  - ➤ If you have time, enroll in short courses on automotive. This will be very handy when you need to purchase a car.

Proof of residency was our second chicken or egg situation. Together with getting our driver's license, we needed to establish our proof of residency.

One of the best things that worked in our favor was Rudy's already getting clearance for his job. He sent us a copy of his employment contract to show proof that we had capacity to pay the monthly rent and all other recurring bills.

- ❖ LESSONS LEARNED
  - ➤ We can't stress enough the importance of friends and family support. Nurture and develop a healthy relationship with them. You never know when you'll need their help.
  - ➤ Treat all people with dignity, especially in their lowest point.
  - ➤ Lend a helping hand without expecting anything in return.

Building your credit score is another major issue in our transition. It's an important process, and it reflects your way of life.

Credit scores represent the credit worthiness of an individual. It's our proof that we pay our bills and aren't dependent on the government or other individuals for financial help. But don't get discourage; it's easy to build your credit score if you're careful and smart in handling your financial transactions.

❖ LESSON LEARNED
   ➢ Prudence and wise spending are important in building your good credit score.

As mentioned earlier, we are here because we want to give the best to our children.

Who would have thought that Dave had a rare medical condition that fortunately was detected and addressed ahead of time through modern medical technology and early intervention?

In January 2019, Dave had a seizure and was diagnosed to have Chiari malformation or brain hernia, which caused elevated blood pressure and involuntary head and muscle movements. If it hadn't been for health care insurance and topnotch medical specialists and facilities, he could have died the same way as our two young brothers. Truly, it was a blessing that we were already in America when it happened.

Dave is now working as a kitchen crew member in a U.S. Navy training facility near our home. He's earning his keep and contributes to our household expenses. At times, he sends money to the Philippines to help his grandparents with their medical expenses. He's trying to save enough to return to school and study culinary arts. He wants to get licensed as a chef to work on a cruise ship.

Daniel, our eldest, who has loved cars since he was two years old, works at a car dealership. He's helped us built our home and enjoys exploring places. He wants to start his own business and continue helping Filipino immigrants achieve their American dream.

As for Rudy, he still works for the State Department as budget analyst. Whenever he can, he takes photos of different sites and events and gets to walk and run to stay fit. He keeps himself up to date with technology and computer programs that helps him with his work and hobbies. He gets to relax and enjoy simple pleasures with our boys.

As for me, I've found a true sense of independence and discovered that despite my vulnerabilities, I'm a strong person. I now work with the City of Charleston after a short stint with retail industry. I've regained my self-confidence and ready to face new challenges in life with my family beside me.

We have different motives and approaches to achieve our dreams. All the experiences that we've gone through and continue to undergo are blessings that we'll be forever grateful for the rest of our lives. We have crossed the bridge of uncertainties and were able to show our children the importance of family and true value of hard work.

Rudy and I are both confident that we made the right decision to leave our comfort zone and pursue the American dream for us and our boys.

6

LORNA FARIÑAS

Procurement Agent
Contracting and Procurement, General Services Office
26 years of service

Optimism is hoping and believing that life gets better. It's having courage and faith in challenging times. Lorna has passed the tests of time. She wasn't discouraged, and she chose to fight.

My journey from preparing a deli sandwich as a salesclerk at Kroger grocery store to being a program analyst with General Services Administration of the federal government was a bumpy yet successful ride.

Here's my story:

I arrived in April 2010 in Wyandotte, Michigan and stayed with my sister's house while looking for a job. It's frustrating in the beginning because it's hard to find a job in the area if there's no one to recommend

you.   Fortunately, after two months, my sister's friend recommended me for a part-time salesclerk job at Kroger.

As soon as I got that job, I rented an apartment and shared it with my friend, Evelyn and her son, who also immigrated almost the same time as me.

Do you imagine walking an hour to and from your work? It's hard, but I did it for four months. I had no car and there was no public transportation in the area. On some days, when I finished late at night, I took a taxi going home. It's a lot of sacrifice, but I enjoyed my job preparing sandwiches. I learned a new skill while practicing my skills in resilience.

I continue searching for a better job. Evelyn and I joined effort in calling our friends and former colleagues to ask for work opportunities. Unfortunately, we didn't get the help we we're hoping for.

In October that year, we finally received the good news that has changed our temporary lives.

Evelyn received a job offer for an administrative position in Washington, D.C. She flew to Maryland to find out about the opportunity. I gave my resume to her in case there was an available position for me.

She was hired as contract specialist instead of an administrative position. While looking for a permanent place, she stayed at her friend's house. When she received her first salary, she rented a basement apartment in Maryland, and told me to relocate with her.

I resigned after Thanksgiving, packed my belongings, and rented a U-Haul truck. A generous coworker offered to drive the truck. The eight-hour drive from Michigan to Maryland was long but opened a new chapter in my life.

After a week of living in Maryland, I was surprised to receive a call from a contractor of the federal government for a job offer. I found out from Evelyn that I was recommended by her boss for the administrative position that was initially offered to her. I took the job of a secretary. Signing my first employment contract with the government was a memorable day.

Life surprises us with occasional challenges. In September 2011, I was diagnosed with breast cancer.

I went through surgery. Unfortunately, my insurance didn't cover all the medical expenses. In addition to dealing with the pain of my physical condition, I was also dealing with my financial situation. To cure my cancer, I needed to undergo radiation for two months at a hospital in Washington, D.C. They informed me that my insurance was exhausted, and I had to spend $8,000.00 out of pocket. They gave me the option to pay my bill on an installment basis.

After further thought, I decided to have my treatment done in the Philippines; the cost was less expensive. My doctor approved my proposal and my supervisor assured me that I would keep my position when I came back.

I received my treatment at the hospital in Manila. After a short recovery, I flew back to America and started working for a new contractor.

After I become an American citizen in September 2015, I started to look for a direct hire position. My supervisor learned about my plan and was worried about losing me at the job. She encouraged me to avail myself of the government disability program, given my cancer condition.

I submitted my disability certificate and resumé to the human resources office. Subsequently, they offered me a position as a building management specialist, but I declined due to compensation issue. With the help of my supervisor, I was hired as a program analyst. After two years, I was promoted and have reached the highest level of my position. I am happy and grateful for my job.

My lack of a college degree wasn't a hindrance to continue my career with the government. I am fortunate for this opportunity. I used my previous work experience, dedication, and hard work as my assets.

When I was deciding to take advantage of the SIV opportunity, some relatives discouraged me to live in America. I didn't listen to them and followed my desire.

I am now cancer free.

Overcoming my disability helped me arrived at the place where I am now. It didn't stop me from moving to where I wanted to go. Rather, I used it as my ladder to reach the top and achieve my goals. Most important, it gave me the strength and courage I needed.

I am grateful for the SIV opportunity, and to the people who helped me on this journey. In two more years, I plan to retire and enjoy my retirement years.

Be positive and resilient. You'll need a lot of these qualities on your journey to SIV.

7

WILLIE PARAN

Computer Management Assistant
Information System Center, Information Management Office
25 years of service

ROUSEL PARAN

Shipment Assistant
Transportation Unit, General Services Office
23 years of service

The success of our children is our success. Providing them with a great opportunity and education will guide them to the right path. When the road gets bumpy, just stay focused. And remember to enjoy the ride. Willie and Rousel love to find adventures. Their life's journey has been successful and fun.

W hen we dream, we dream big! To immigrate in America is not easy as counting 1, 2, 3. It's heartbreaking to leave a good life, good friends, and a stable job at the embassy. However, the SIV opportunity we earned was a sweet reward for our dedication and loyalty with the American government.

Willie and I have served the U.S. Government for a combined forty-eight years. Our careers started at the U.S. Naval Base where we met.

It's more of mixed feelings for Willie and myself, but the excitement and enthusiasm of our kids were clear. Even though the skepticism sometimes popped in, we were ready to face the future.

Our journey began in 2007 when Willie and I with our two teenage sons immigrated to the East Coast, New Jersey. We had a long vacation to enjoy the new environment.

We arrived during "the 2008 great recession in U.S. history." Finding a job was hard. My first work at a retail store lasted for only two days. I resigned because it wasn't what I wanted to do. But I enjoyed the people I worked with.

I was hired by two government offices; the first one was the U.S. Postal Office, and the second was the New York State Housing Authority. I also worked for a technology company, and  the recent one is a big conglomerate snack company. I've tried various positions, and that gave me multiple skills and experiences.

Willie's first job was with a financial technology company. He started as a check sorter operator, eventually transferred to the computer data center. He worked in California for two years in pursuit of his information technology career. Fortunately, he regained his career with the government and he's back doing what he loves as an IT professional. He works for the Federal Emergency Management Agency, where he travels to other states for his job; that's the exciting part of his profession.

The good education of our sons is one blessing we are grateful for. They earned their college degrees from top universities in New Jersey. Our older, Darryl is a graduate of sociology from Montclair University with a career in health care. My younger son, Francis, finished his degree in information technology from Rutgers University. They are both successful in their chosen careers and work in one of the best cities in the world, New York City.

We have a different outlook as individuals and as a family. We differ in the way we enjoy our lives. My family enjoys traveling and exploring. I make sure we travel every year and every occasion to celebrate. We do long drives, including cross-country drives. This is one of the best things we enjoy as a family, and one of the best perks we have in America.

Immigrating is taking a risk, with the ups and downs of life. But the best part of this journey is the many happy and exciting escapades.

Our best advice to future special visa immigrants: Enjoy the ride, be grateful and, as our former boss said, "Don't look back."

8

MARILEE JOY MANCAO-PASANDALAN

Secretary
Cultural Affairs Office
25 years of service

We are all dreamers. We are all achievers. Don't let adversity stop you from believing that you're capable of making that dream come true. Joy was inspired and found herself no longer dreaming. She's a dreamer, a believer, and a survivor.

I've always dreamt that, someday, I could visit and stay in California. After retiring, I traveled to America in January 2018 for the first time. I fell in love with California, the beauty and people around me. Since my first visit, I went back three times.

My former colleagues welcomed me and encouraged me to apply for SIV. I was convinced and

immediately started the process.

I made my way back to California in September 2019. I was proud to be back as a permanent resident. A thick binder of my SIV portfolio, resume, immigration documents, and two heavy suitcases were my important belongings I carried with me.

The immigration officers and the staff at the airport were all nice. They gave me a warm welcome as a new immigrant. I felt that I belong in this country.

I am grateful for the love and support of friends from our fraternity and sorority group. They paid for my plane ticket and initial accommodations. Having this kind of huge help made my transition less stressful. They are my family and inspiration.

Living in America without children and being unwell can be a tough situation. In my case, I make it less difficult by keeping a positive outlook. As I start a new life, I also begin a new challenge.

I was diagnosed with breast cancer in March 2019.

My priority is to heal myself. I'm ready to work when a job opportunity arrives. Meanwhile, I continue to enjoy my social life, visiting friends and relatives and meeting former colleagues. In California, we have an active group of retirees from the American Embassy with whom I communicate often and do fun things. I'm blessed to have this inner circle of people guiding me on this new journey.

All my children are grown up. But I also have a dream for them to experience the American life someday. I didn't give my children the choice earlier, but it's not too late.

My twenty-five years working for the Cultural Affairs Office was a great career. I showed up to the office every day with enthusiasm, pride, and joy. The experiences I've gained, skills I've learned, and friends I've developed made me who I am now.

Retirement means starting to design a new life. We want to start or continue a hobby. We want to take care or see our grandkids often. We want to visit more friends and relatives. We want to travel more. We want to use our retirement years to enjoy more of our lives.

I'm designing a new life now, healing myself. California is my new home where I found a new hope and a new beginning. I'm grateful for the SIV opportunity making this happen.

My story is inspired by my favorite song: "California Dreaming" by The Mamas and the Papas. I am quoting few lines to remind myself that I'm no longer dreaming.

"All the leaves are brown, and the sky is gray.

I've been for a walk on a winter's day.

I'd be safe and warm if I was in LA.

California dreamin' on such a winters day."

Believe in your dreams. Make them happen.

9

JOJIE SOPIA

Cultural Affairs Assistant
Public Affairs Office
25 years of service

Success is a personal thing. If you love where you are, or you love what you do, then you're successful. Jojie's perspective of success makes her a successful SIV story. Her enormous faith led her to where she is and continues to guide her with happiness and contentment.

"How to be successful" is a popular topic and question. We gather tips and seek advice from people. We read books and do research. Most of us use education, skills, abilities, talents, and experiences. We keep a positive attitude and maintain focus. These are some contributing factors for a successful career and successful life.

But there's more than that.

My decision to immigrate to America was primarily to open a new chapter of my life.

I left the Philippines in September 2010 and stayed with my former colleague and friend in Virginia. I love Virginia but I'm not a fan of winter. So, in December, I moved to Nevada and stayed with another friend.

I had a great experience working for twenty-five years at the American Embassy. There's no dull moment. I miss that job, my friends, and family. I also miss my lifestyle, especially the fun of shopping.

However, it was time for a change and time to explore. I gave up my stable job and my comfortable life in the Philippines.

The culture we experienced at the embassy is a foundation that we can use to help us in our transition. However, life here can be different. It's hard to find a job, especially when you're new. You must also be tough dealing with the experience.

We have different definitions of success. My definition of success is being happy. I am happy where I am now. The company of my friends makes life exciting. I have their emotional support that I miss from my relatives and friends in the Philippines.

I love the weather in Nevada and the fun things we do in Las Vegas. I enjoy my job and having a simple life with the grace of God.

Here's a favorite piece of wisdom that serves as a reminder for me and for other believers:

"You will become successful not because of your skill but because of the grace of God."

Don't give up and have faith.

10

JUN ENALPE

Chief Engineer
Facilities Management Office
Overseas Building Operations
23 years of service

Take advantage of opportunities you encounter. That big opportunity may be right in front of you. Use them as stepping-stones to reach your goal. When you change your thoughts, you have the unlimited power to achieve. Jun was in the right time and had the right opportunity. He changed his mindset. It not only opened more opportunities but also opened the door for achievements.

Sometime in 2010, my wife and I had a conversation about what we could do for the future of our children. We came up with the idea of bringing them to America to give them better options. We used to joke that we might not get the job we used to have. Instead, we could be working together in a building as a janitor and janitress. That's the mindset we had.

That same year, I had an opportunity to attend training in Washington D.C. I told my wife to join me and see for herself if

41

we should venture to start a new life in America. After the training, we decided to go for it.

In 2013, I was to receive an award from the State Department. I used that opportunity to look for a job. I sought help from my former colleagues as well as friends from the State Department.

During my ten days in the Washington D.C. area, three companies responded to my job applications.

A company in Washington D.C. interviewed me in person. I was offered a job in Iraq. Consequently, I declined the offer, as it defeated the purpose of my family living together in America.

Another company located in Virginia interviewed me over the phone and invited me to come in person to discuss the possible benefits.

Tidewater Inc. in Maryland, a contractor of the Overseas Buildings Operations of the federal government, reached out to me. I attended a seminar in Construction Quality Management to  get a certificate required for the job. The seminar was administered by Naval Facilities and U.S. Army Corps of Engineers. Most things were familiar to me. I was thankful for my previous experience. I passed the certification and interview, was hired, and the rest is history.

We immigrated in 2014. My 17-year-old son was excited, while my 20-year-old son was hesitant and wanted to stay in the Philippines. Eventually, I convinced him. We compromised with the caveat that he could go back if he didn't like living in America.

I started with Tidewater Inc. as a project engineer, then later promoted to a task manager. My current position as a project manager gives me the opportunity to travel. So far, I've visited eighteen American embassies and consulates worldwide.

My previous negative mindset to get a job as a janitor was proven wrong. I changed my mindset. I acknowledged the opportunity given to me and took advantage of it.

I gave my sons the same opportunity I received from the government, by bringing them to America. My son who previously wanted to stay in the Philippines is happy where he's now.

Aim high but don't expect too much.

11

CECILLE CANLAS

Financial and Administrative Specialist
U.S. Commercial Service, Department of Commerce
23 years of service

A genuine story of success comes from a humble beginning. Consistent hard work, great determination, combined with a large amount of faith will lead you to the right path. Cecille's journey was long and bumpy, but she was patient and determined to get to her destination. She has also proven that dreams do come true.

When I was young, I dreamt of living in America. But how? I wasn't even sure if I could finish college and don't have a family to file an immigrant petition for us. Through hard work, I finished college and was fortunate enough to get a job at the American Embassy.

In January 2010, we made it to the "Land of Milk and Honey."

I told myself, "This is it. We have a new life, a new beginning." To have a better future for my family was my goal. But we arrived during the time America was in a recession. Our transition wasn't easy.

A relative in New Jersey adopted us for a few months. Some things didn't work out well. Finding a job was hard. Eventually, all my resources were used up; We received some help from relatives and friends. During that time, I was supporting my two daughters who were studying in the Philippines. It was a challenging time.

After 5 months, another relative invited us to Las Vegas to explore opportunities. I was more determined and motivated. We packed our bags and took a bus ride that lasted for more than 2 days. It was a long journey, yet the start of many triumphs.

There are many job opportunities in Las Vegas if you're not picky. My first job was a bus person at a famous diner. I also became a caregiver for a short time. Later, I got a job at a posh hotel, the Venetian Resort and Casino, as a housekeeper. This job was hard; I found myself crying almost every single day, as I had to clean 11 rooms daily. The only thing that kept me going was the good compensation to support my family. Providing for my family is all that matters to me.

A great opportunity was offered to me as a supervisor at the Venetian Resort and Casino. It's been 9 years now, and I still recall the challenging time when I did the housekeeping job. To start from an entry-level position is a good way to start. A better opportunity will come when the time is right. Be humble and patient.

My family is now doing well and keeps on growing. My two older daughters are now married with stable jobs, and a new addition to the family is coming soon. My third daughter has a good job in the medical field. And my youngest daughter who has always been the pride of my family, graduated as a valedictorian in high school. She's a scholar studying biomedical engineering at the University of Nevada.

All my struggles and frustrations have paid off. I wouldn't ask for anything more. I'm blessed with a new life in America. It's a good life as a result of determination, hard work, and faith.

My childhood dream was to live in America. It's now a reality. Just believe in God that He will not forsake you, and be a good person.

12

RENATO VEGA

Administrative Assistant
Public Affairs Office
22 years of service

Great things come from hard work. Allow yourself to step down and make a goal to move up. Nato started from the bottom. Now, he's enjoying the fruits of his labor. He also knows the rule of work hard and have fun.

I immigrated to America for my family. We arrived in February 2012 and settled in New Jersey. My first job was a part-time janitor at Dunkin Donuts for four months. It was a decent job and I wasn't embarrassed doing it.

After working for Dunkin Donuts, I was hired at a nursing home in the laundry department. A memorable experience happened when I found a fire, worked to prevent its spread, and called 911 for assistance. That incident saved the lives of the residents in the nursing home. I was honored when management gave me an "employee of the month" award to recognize me.

I moved from the nursing home to a hospital job. I started as a janitor for a year, then was later promoted to a case pick position. My responsibility was to prepare supplies for the operating rooms. This job lasted for four years and gave me the experience I needed.

I never expected I would get the job that I have now. As an anesthesia technician for a prestigious hospital, I assist doctors with supplies and medicine they need for the operating rooms. I also troubleshoot anesthesia machines and supervise four staff. The hospital trained and trusted me to do this job that I've been doing for two years now.

My skill as a massage therapist in the Philippines was a big advantage. I became more adept and elevated my skill to a therapeutic massage level. My clients have grown, and I visit them for home service. Helping people by being a therapeutic massage therapist is one of the best things that happened to me in America.

I'm happy and thankful that I gave my two daughters better opportunities through the SIV program. My oldest daughter, Izza, is a registered nurse at a private hospital in New York. While my younger daughter, Jeska, is finishing her nursing degree.

The best thing about working hard is to anticipate having fun as well. I work hard, and we go to the Philippines for vacation and visit relatives once a year.

There are good things about living America. One thing is the equal opportunity we enjoy in both aspects of work and life.

Work hard and focus. Ask questions if you need to. Speak up if you have the right. Don't complain if it's not worth complaining about.

In America, you just need to work and you won't go hungry. There are many opportunities available if you're willing to try. Don't be embarrassed to have a menial job. Strive to work your way up.

Also, be prepared and expect the unexpected.

13

YNA QUIAMBAO

Commercial Specialist
U.S. Commercial Service, Department of Commerce
22 years of service

Gratitude and humility go hand in hand. Having these two together means putting yourself into a faster lane with more blessings and accomplishments. Yna has helped many American companies on her previous job. She's now humbled by receiving more grace. Her grateful heart and enormous faith have always been her powers in achieving great things and receiving more blessings.

"An Experience of Many Firsts." My career with the American Embassy is one of the greatest blessings of my life. I graduated at age 20 and after a three-month contract with the U.S. Commercial Service, a permanent position opened. The rest is history.

I love what we do at the U.S. Commercial Service - "diplomacy through trade" - bringing American exports to the

Philippines to create jobs in America and business opportunities for Filipinos. I was responsible for defense, information communication technology, and transportation portfolios. I thrived in helping them find ways to sell and I was proud to represent some of the largest American companies.

The decision to apply for SIV wasn't an easy one, given how I enjoyed and was very passionate about the work that I do. I knew I would give up my career to explore the unknown.

My children, seven-year-old Josh and four-year-old Faith, were the reasons I applied for SIV. As my husband, Leo, puts it, we had the opportunity to live our lives and pursue careers we enjoyed. The SIV was an opportunity to expand the options that will be available for our children. American education will open more doors for them.

I submitted my SIV application in March 2018 and received approval after six months. We started working on our documents in January 2019 and were hoping to leave the middle of the year. I faced a lot of delays with visa issuance, and our medical clearance was put into risk. Our visa was finally issued on October 2, we left on October 12, and our medical clearance was due to expire on October 17! Everything was in the nick of time.

We landed in Houston, Texas and stayed with my first cousin and her family. At first, my husband and I planned to go about this whole process on our own. We didn't want to bother anyone because we were a family of four and would be a burden. When I informed my cousin about our upcoming migration, she invited us to stay with her family in Texas as we got settled.

We're blessed to have relatives who welcomed us with open arms and were willing and able to help. I'm amazed and humbled at their kindness and generosity. They're not only providing lodging but also practical advice about building a life in America and holding our hands through this process. We're awed by God's goodness manifested through my cousins.

So far, things are coming together for us, one by one. Our children were able to go to school a week after we arrived. I couldn't believe how fast and efficient the school application was.

We received our social security numbers and permanent resident cards the same month we arrived. This allowed us to open a bank account and acquire a driver's license.

Leo went to his first job interview at MD Anderson in early December and was immediately hired. My cousin's referral greatly helped. With Leo's new job, we saw the need to purchase a vehicle. Initially, we tried to buy a car on our own, but it didn't work out since we had no credit history. My cousin offered to cosign to help us get a better deal. With her help, we were able to buy our first car.

I have started looking into job options for myself, as we're also trying to figure out childcare should both of us work. The cost of after school care in Texas ranges from $150-250 per week for a child, depending on age and how much time the child spends at the facility. I reflect on what I want to do now - work or stay at home with the kids. My domestic skills leave much to be desired but spending more time with them has given me so much joy. Perhaps this is what I must do for now. As my former boss and a good friend described it well; "You're finding your sync."

One of our favorite priests always says that, in life, we shouldn't stop growing and learning. He used to ask me this question: "When was the last time you did something for the first time?" For a long time, I couldn't answer that question because I was in my comfort zone.

Now, everything is a first! I understand even more the importance of doing things for the first time - apart from keeping your mind alert, you become aware of your own nothingness and become more dependent on the Grace of God.

Here are some practical tips to consider: If you have young children, find a good school and secure a slot for your children as soon as possible. Public schools will accept students at any time during the school year. To have someone as a guarantor can fast-track your ability to buy a car or rent an apartment. Find the best deal - always. Research, negotiate, and don't be embarrassed to say no.

Finally, this SIV journey has taught me two important lessons:

First: Embracing change. Take on the new adventure and instead of allowing fear to rule - have faith. The Lord won't take you where His Grace cannot sustain you.

Second: Humility. Learn to ask for and receive help. You're used to being independent but when you immigrate to America, you need as much help as you can get.

As I was told, "Just accept the help given to you; it's a blessing."

14

BENNY QUEÑANO

Protocol Assistant
Protocol Office
22 years of service

Fear stops you from achieving. Faith is a way to overcome that fear.
Benny was guided by faith and a positive attitude. It led him to his
choice of destination, where he's happy and grateful.

America! As the old folks say, it's the land of milk and honey. Many of us can't deny that we love America. After graduating from college, I got my first job working for the American government at Clark Air Force Base. The unfortunate eruption of Mt. Pinatubo in 1991 had caused the closure of the base that subsequently ended my career as well.

I was fortunate to join the U.S. mission again in 1998 at the American Embassy as a telephone operator.

In 2001, upon the request of the ambassador, I was chosen by the chief of the Information Management Office to be responsible for screening the incoming calls of the Office of the Chief of Mission. Eventually, I was promoted and became a Protocol Office staff.

I've never dreamt of immigrating to America, even though I was already working for the government. My parents, siblings, and their families residing in America never encouraged me to come. It came to a point when I had to decide if I would try my luck and apply for SIV before my daughter turned 21 years old. My decision was also influenced by an American colleague who suggested that I should consider it.

Fast forward and after receiving the approval of my application and going through the entire immigration process, I resigned from what I consider my "best job," which I miss. My family and I left the Philippines in June 2012.

Leaving the country where I lived for 50 years wasn't easy. It was even harder for my daughter, who only had one more year to finish her college degree.

It's exciting to learn and adapt to a new life in a foreign land. However, there's always the fear from asking yourself, "What if?"

Overcoming doubts about whether I would be able to have a better and successful life in America takes a lot of courage. Reality awaits you.

We resided in California for six months. To have family members and relatives ready to help us in every way, to guide us, and to provide the necessary means to survive was an advantage.

We also met good people and old friends from the Philippines who were ready to help. We're truly grateful.

I'm a very positive person. I tried not to focus on the fear of not making it. I'll never forget when I told my wife and daughter, "God will not bring us to America if He doesn't have a good plan for us."

One day, when I was getting ready to search for a job, a very good friend called and invited me to watch a boxing fight in Las Vegas. We drove to Vegas, met up with friends, attended a prayer meeting with the "Champ" and his family, had boxing gloves autographed, and explored Las Vegas.

That was my turning point.

On our way back to California, I decided that Las Vegas was the place for me and my family to settle. It wasn't because we love city life, but I believed that this city had so much more to offer. The city's public transportation system was round the clock, so navigating without a car was easy. More importantly, I could easily find a job. Therefore, my family and I returned to Las Vegas with a new beginning.

I was blessed to get a job easily. However, I didn't work too long at my first job before I found a better one that I love. I've been working there for almost seven years. Our life is more comfortable now than the first six months we arrived.

We love living in America.

When you're planning to immigrate, be prepared. Don't be picky in getting your first job. Employers prefer to hire someone with local experience. You can easily move from one job to another. Be assertive and have an open mind.

If you believe that you have the ability and the right attitude to do what it takes to succeed in America, then go for it. Your success is in your own hands. Best of luck to you.

Finally, if you chose to reside in Las Vegas, send me a message. I'm glad to assist and help you in any way.

15

JACKIE REYES

Coach
Veterans Service Center, U.S. Department of Veterans Affairs
22 years of service

*Change is inevitable. When it happens, face it with courage and
learn how to grow from the experience. Jackie has gone through
some changes in life, including her job and decisions. She was able to
cope with it courageously and used it to her advantage.*

To live in America was not my dream until I was hired by the Department of Veterans Affairs in May 1989. Things change, as well as perspective.

I started having a desire to live in America when I reached

my fifteenth year of service. On my twentieth year, I thought to pursue my desire. My family and I left the Philippines in August 2011 to begin a new life in Jacksonville, Florida.

It was a life-changing decision.

I have no relatives in America, so leaving my father and siblings in the Philippines was emotionally hard. Resigning from a high-paying job was also a big risk financially.

I didn't wait long to get a job with the government. I was hired as a call center agent with the Department of Children and Families in December 2011.

The communication barrier dealing with very demanding and irate clients, learning new information, and adjusting to the new culture were part of the struggles I encountered. I used my training, skills, and experience from the Department of Veterans Affairs in dealing with the kind of clientele we served.

I've exceeded my performance expectations and was given the privilege to work from home for more than a year. I enjoyed the experience, having the biggest perk of not getting up early to arrive in the office at eight o'clock.

Eventually, a mentor position became available. I applied and was promoted to the position.

Before I left the Philippines, I told myself that I would never work again as a supervisor, because it's a demanding and stressful job. But just like what I've said earlier, things change and decisions change. A supervisor position was offered to me by the director of the agency. I grabbed the opportunity and, now, I'm on my fourth year as a supervisor.

My job has exposed me to different government agencies and local community partners that provide food, medical, shelter, utility, unemployment, and temporary cash assistance to low-income families. Dealing with this every day is a humble experience. It makes me more grateful for the life I have.

I was fortunate to attain one of the highest positions at the Department of Veterans Affairs and realized that I still had enough room to learn and grow. It's been eight years since I started working with the Department of Children and Families agency. I've learned a lot and I'm still enjoying my job.

If an opportunity comes to work for the Department of Veterans Affairs, where my heart really belongs, I would be glad to take the chance again.

My piece of advice to someone who will take advantage of the SIV - go for it; it's worth the plunge. I also encourage you to start saving before making that big decision.

16

LUNINGNING MERCADO

Visa Assistant/Team Leader - Special Action Team
Immigrant Visa, Consular Office
21 years of service

*Having a sense of mission brings out a sense of gratification. The
size of your mission is not as important as the sincerity of your
intention. Ning Ning was tasked to perform many missions. She has
accomplished them with a grateful heart
and a sense of fulfillment.*

Missions Accomplished! My previous jobs with the American government have helped me accomplish my purpose in life. I gave my heart in performing those jobs and, in return, I received the feeling of gratification in making a difference to other people's lives.

To assist Vietnamese refugees find a new country to settle in was a humbling job. With empathy and commitment, I single-handedly managed the resettlement process of more than two thousand remaining Vietnamese Amerasians, refugees, and long-stayers. For sixteen years, 229 Vietnamese refugees lived in the Philippines without a permanent status but their journey to a new home ended when they arrived in America on a chartered flight. I ended the program in 2008 with mixed emotions of happiness, relief, and sadness of missing the program.

Adoption, being one of the top priorities in the Department of State, requires speedy attention and accuracy in the immigrant visa process. Assisting orphans to find a new family and home was comforting. My community service for the orphanages started in 2009, which eventually turned out to be an annual "Diaper Drive." It benefited local orphanages and enhanced the public image of the Immigrant Visa Section. I helped to make the American Embassy Philippines a model post for "The Hague Adoption Process" in Asia. It was, indeed, a fulfilling job.

To facilitate the special immigrant visa applicants, begin a new life in America was a motivating experience. Since 2001, I handled the SIV applications for employees. This includes employees from the naval bases in the Philippines and Diego Garcia, and Filipino employed staff in American embassies in other countries. I streamlined the process, organized orientations to educate prospective applicants on the procedural and documentary requirements, selection criteria, and regulations. I acted as secretary of the panel review board and managed into conclusion all applications after the panel review. It has brought me joy seeing my colleagues happy and grateful for the SIV blessing. This experience has ended with my own application.

Yet, I had a bigger mission.

I was guided to the path where I adopted my two grandchildren. They are the daughters of my only son. My purpose was to bring them to America as my dependents. It was a long process, but the outcome was worth the wait.

We immigrated in 2015 and stayed with relatives in California. My daughters, Kyla, now 20 years old, is in college, pursuing a nursing degree, and Kline who is 17 years old and in the 11th grade, wants to be a nurse as well. Both are high achievers in school, and they make me proud.

As a mother, I instill in their minds to keep the Filipino culture and values. I always remind them to prioritize their studies. They both understand the reason I adopted them and brought them in America was for their brighter and better future. I do believe they can achieve it.

We love the way of living in America. We appreciate the discipline of people on the road, the cleanliness of the environment and the diversity of food. As young ladies, Kyla and Kline love new trends in make-up, hair style, wardrobe, shoes, bags, and everything about beauty and fashion. These are the things they enjoy.

I miss my son, my relatives, and friends in the Philippines. I also miss my house and some Filipino food. We've gone through a lot of changes, but we all realize it's for the best.

My family is now settled in. I'm happy and contented with the life I have. Taking care of my children is my priority.

Traveling is fun and I'm looking forward to see more of this beautiful country in the near future.

I used to bid goodbye to my former colleagues who were grateful for my guidance in facilitating their SIV. Now, I'm one of them - living a new life I chose.

The SIV was my world for years. It became my foundation, and eventually ended my journey at the embassy. I'm grateful to be a part of this wonderful opportunity.

Family and real friends are there to support you in many ways. Count your blessings and be grateful, always.

My life is a journey of many missions, and I am glad to accomplish them.

17

VIRGILIO LINGLING

Communication Clerk
Document Communication Services
Information Management Office
21 years of service

Sacrifice is a part of life. Yet beyond that sacrifice is the anticipation that something good is waiting in the horizon. Ver is making that sacrifice being away from his children. He was rewarded with a job that allows him to see them and hopes that, someday, they'll be together again.

To leave my four children behind was the hardest part of my decision to immigrate. They were too old and could no longer join me. Despite the hesitation, I left the Philippines in March 2015 with my wife. It broke my heart, but I pursued my dream.

Having friends in America to guide and support you is a blessing. To know that someone will accommodate you at their house for the first few weeks or months helps you during your transition. It lessens your worries while you try to build a new life. In our case, we stayed with a former colleague and friend, Alex, until we became established and bought our own house.

We have a group of former embassy employees in Washington D.C. and Virginia with whom we socialize. We have a regular "Sabado (Saturday) nights" to unwind after a week of hard work. It seems like we haven't left the Philippines. It is our version of "Thank God It's Friday" nights at the embassy.

I was lucky to get my first job in June 2015 as part-time cabin agent with DAL Global Services. My wife and I enjoy the wonderful privilege of traveling to the Philippines on standby status to visit my children. I'm thankful for this benefit because it gives me easy access to visit them.

My full-time job now as general clerk with Pacific Architecture Engineering, a contractor of a diplomatic pouch for government facilities, is the right path to regain my government career. I enjoy what I do and continue to seek a better opportunity.

The physical absence of our children and grandchildren is the downside of living in America, but I don't have regrets. Thanks to modern technology and my travel benefit, I can visit them virtually and in person.

Take advantage of what you have. Make the most of everything.

18

RENNIE DEL ROSARIO

Laboratory Animal House Supervisor
U.S. Naval and Medical Research Unit No. 2
3 years of service

HAZEL DEL ROSARIO

Human Resources Assistant
Human Resources Office
20 years of service

The challenge you overcome only makes you stronger, and your faith gets bigger. Rennie and Hazel were tested with a challenge that surprised them. But the amount of resilience they have was enough to rise above that challenge with courage, grace, and gratefulness in their hearts.

Are we going to be okay? This big question was bothering me ever since we left the Philippines in July 2007 to immigrate in America.

It was Rennie's idea to live here. I was apprehensive to pursue my application for the special immigrant visa program because we had a comfortable life back home, not to mention we're leaving behind families and good friends. But not everybody has the privilege to apply for the SIV program. Rennie was convinced that our kids would have a better future.

We landed in Los Angeles, California, with five suitcases to start a new life. My daughter Nikka, was 12 years old and my younger son Julian, was 6 years old. With a heavy heart, we left my older son Raphael, who was 16, to  finish high school. Leaving Raphael behind wasn't easy. He didn't like the idea of moving here and it was tough to finally convinced him. We left him with one condition, that he would follow as soon as he graduated.

Life is a series of changes.

Our plan to live in California didn't materialize. After two weeks in Los Angeles, we were invited by a friend to check out Goodyear, Arizona. We immediately fell in love with the place. We believe that Goodyear is a better place to raise our kids. We do believe that we made a good choice.

We arrived during the time of recession when life and finding a job were difficult.

Fortunately, a month after our arrival in Arizona, we were both hired as contract employees with the State of Arizona. Two months later, I was offered a full-time position at the Attorney General's Office. I believe the experience and professional growth I've gained while working at the embassy has helped me get interviews with government positions. I was lucky to have the opportunity to choose between two government job offers. Up to this date, I am happy working at the Attorney General's Office as a legal assistant.

Rennie was a veterinarian back home. His goal was to find a job in his line of work. He was hired as a dialysis technician after his contract position with the State. But soon after, he realized this job wasn't a good fit for him. He now works as a senior animal health technician at the County Animal Shelter.

Then something unfortunate happened.

After being here for a little over a year, Rennie was diagnosed with soft tissue Sarcoma, a rare form of cancer. We were shocked, devastated, and I felt so hopeless. We had to deal with it with strength and courage. It has tested our faith, and our family became stronger. I recall those days when I was crying at work every day. I was thankful to have a supportive supervisor and friends who helped us cope emotionally.

Rennie's surgery and treatments were costly. Luckily, my health insurance at work has covered everything. This was one reason we say that we made a good decision to move to America. It could have been a different situation and financially stressful if this had happened in the Philippines. It has been twelve years since he was diagnosed, and I thank God every day for His healing miracles.

It was a challenge to leave the life we had been accustomed to.

There's no more household help nor families who could help us take care of our children, especially Jullian. All four of us had to make big adjustments during our first few years. We had to use the after-school program so someone could take care of Jullian while we were still at work. Rennie and I would rush to the school after work to pick him up. Our mornings were also challenging, since we had to leave early for work. My daughter was a tremendous help to us. She would help him get ready for school and walk him to the school bus pick up area every day. It hurts us to see that Nikka, at a very young age, was tasked with looking after her 6-year-old brother as they were very sheltered growing up in the Philippines.

Nikka's transition from being a shy kid has changed a lot when she joined the talent show at school. Her talent in singing has helped her transition and develop her personality. She joined the church choir at the age of 12 and continues to sing. She also sings at weddings, Filipino festivities, and other events.

Nikka had an internship with the U.S. Secret Service in college. She finished a degree in business, majoring in global politics at the Arizona State University. She now works at one of the world's largest investment companies. We're proud that she'll soon finish her master's in business administration.

As planned, our oldest son, Raphael came after he graduated from high school. He worked part time for two years while pursuing his associate degree. Because of that, he's learned the value of hard work and saving money. Raphael finished his business degree in sustainability at the Arizona State University and associate degree in computer information systems at Estrella

Mountain College. While working full time, he managed to take computer certifications which helped him land a job he loves. He works as a systems administrator at a company that runs a restaurant chain nationwide. His plan is to buy a house in a couple of years.

Jullian, who practically grew up here, is now a freshman at the Arizona State University. He plans to pursue a career in the health industry as a physical therapist.

Indeed, our decision to immigrate is a blessing.

In the Philippines, we did enjoy a comfortable life. But in America, we're providing our children with better career opportunities, convenient environment, and a good education. My fear and worries have been replaced with feelings of accomplishments, contentment, and happiness. We're thankful for the SIV opportunity.

From having three children in our household, we are now empty-nesters. Now, it's time to think about us and plan our retirement.

Our piece of advice: Don't be afraid to try it out. There are many available resources and help. If others have done it, you can do it too!

19

VALENTINO CORREA

Driver Clerk
Foreign Commercial Service
Commercial Liaison to Asian Development Bank
20 years of service

Great stories are worth telling. Tiny is a simple person with a complicated yet inspiring life. His past misdemeanors and hardships made him who he is now. He had the courage to fight and a hope that gave light to his obscure road. You can choose the path where you want to go. Tiny made the right decision to change, and it led him to the right path. His story is inspiring and worth telling.

Let me begin by narrating my story of "From rags to a comfortable life." During my teenage years, I was considered the black sheep in the family. I didn't even finish high school. My father used to beat me, hit me with slippers, belt, stick, flat iron cable, 2x2 wooden

pole; punch me with his big fist, and kick me. He told me, "You're not a good son and don't have a bright future."

I had a doubt that my father's abuse all started when he discovered the love affair of my older sister who was his favorite and the brightest among us. She had a relationship with a guy who worked as a cabinet sander in the company where my father worked. My father didn't like him because he believed he wasn't the best man for my sister. He was bitter about it and dump his anger on me.

Every day, I received punishment from my father. He hit me for the slightest mistake to the point that I couldn't take it any longer. One day, while I was eating with my sister, he told me to get a haircut. He didn't like how my hair looked and suddenly grabbed my hair. I lost my mind and stabbed him on his arm. Fortunately, it wasn't fatal or serious. Up to this day, I regret doing that to my father. But I was happy that before he died, we had patched up our relationship.

During those days, I used basketball to vent my anger toward my father. Every day, I was involved in a street fight and was given an alias, "Tibak," which means a hard core in our community. I stayed until dawn drinking and joined guys stealing laundry. In short, I had a bad reputation in our neighborhood.

From then on, I felt a strong inferiority complex. I told myself that maybe I would never have my own family. I often asked myself, "Who would like a guy like me?" I'm not a good-looking guy, but neither am I ugly. Every time I thought how I can provide a future to my family, I thought that marrying wasn't for me.

In the early 80's, I was lucky to work in Jeddah, Saudi Arabia. I told myself that after two years, I would have enough money to buy a passenger "jeepney" and start a family. I sent two-thirds of my salary to the Philippines while my mother kept my bank account. Unfortunately, after fourteen months on the job, the company delayed our salary, until they owed us seven months. Then, I decided to go back home. I found out that the money I sent my mother was used for the education of my youngest sister. My mother wanted to repay me using her retirement money, but I didn't allow her.

That sealed my fate, and I told myself I would just remain single. I had a job, but it wasn't enough to raise a family. My mother told me that it would be hard to grow old alone and no one would take care of me when I got sick.

Fortunately, I got married and soon had a son who was born premature. Both my wife and son were in critical condition when he was born almost died. I didn't know where to get money to pay the hospital bills. I was lucky to have great friends who contributed to pay the bills. It was a hard time to survive, as I got my income daily.

Then I experienced a turning point in my life.

I was on my way to buy milk for my four-month-old son. I computed how much he consumed milk for a week and how much I spent on cigarettes. It cost 200 pesos for the milk and 200 pesos for cigarettes. I was embarrassed with myself; I didn't have enough salary, yet I was competing with my son for his milk. I told myself I should stop smoking now. I threw away the last cigarette in my pocket.

Driving was my bread and butter. I worked for the Philippine Department of Energy and met a consultant from U.S. Agency for International Development, Michael Ellis. He was young, nice, and quiet type guy, but we became friends immediately.

Before I finished my contract with the Department of Energy, I asked him a favor to recommend me for a driver job at the American Embassy. He wrote me a recommendation and sent it to the embassy newsletter. I was then hired as a family driver by the Senior Officer of FCS, Mr. Jonathan Bensky. Before he left the Philippines, I asked him to recommend me to another job at the embassy. This time, I was hired as an office driver by the Head of FCS, Ms. Janet Thomas.

Heaven was slowly opening its door for me.

After working for four months through an employment agency, I requested Ms. Thomas if I could be directly employed by the embassy, instead of going through the agency, which got a cut of my salary. She was nice and approved my request; I became an official employee in March 1993. After a year as a driver, I was promoted to a driver/clerk position, having my own work area, official cell phone, and business card. My job was to send ADB data to American companies.

In a short period, I went from renting a small room to owning two houses. The best part was that we had a comfortable life. My bad reputation had changed, and all I heard were praises from our community. I finally retired in September 2013.

I immigrated February 2015 to Chicago with my daughter who was 19 years old. Unfortunately, I couldn't bring my son, who was already 24 years old. My wife followed me the following year. We're hoping that our son will join us soon.

My first job was a dishwasher at a Filipino restaurant. I also worked at McDonald's in the kitchen crew with my daughter as my supervisor. I became a bagger at a grocery store and a line worker at a pizza company. My current job is a food server with LSG Sky Chef, preparing food and meals for major airlines. My daughter now is a quality assurance worker at a global electronics manufacturing services company.

The success of my life story began not when I arrived in America as an immigrant. It started when a nice American, Mr. Ellis, helped me get a job at the embassy. The SIV was a continuation of my success.

I'm glad to share the real story of my life. It has taught me many lessons and brought me to where I am now. I am thankful for my employment with the American government and for those people who helped me along the way.

The ultimate lessons I've learned that I'd like to share with you: First, don't lose hope. Second, believe in good karma.

20

ALEX FIGUEROA

Motor Vehicle Dispatcher
U.S. Department of Veterans Affairs
20 years of service

Family separation is sometimes inevitable. But they guide you to the right path where it would be beneficial for you. Alex has a unique success story. The history of his sacrifice was the product of his present blessings. He worked hard to make sure his past won't happen again.

My father was also an SIV recipient after retiring with 27 years of service. I was left behind with four of my other siblings because we exceeded the age requirement. My youngest sister was the only one who was qualified to immigrate with him.

As soon as I had my 20th year in service, I applied immediately for SIV. I wanted to make sure that I could bring all my children. I was happy that it happened.

We arrived in June 2012 and stayed with my sister in Chicago. With the invitation of my aunt, we moved to Indiana after a month. I was fortunate to get a job with Purdue University, one of the best aviation universities in America and a company that offers great health benefits. I started as a custodian and am now a preventive maintenance technician. It's a great job that I enjoy. My wife also works for Purdue University as a custodian.

I left the Philippines with mixed emotions. I was happy that I could bring my family and have them experience American life. At the same time, I was sad that I would miss my other siblings. I was also concerned about the change in lifestyle and how we could adapt with it.

Soon after arriving, the initial reaction of my children was to go back to the Philippines. The culture shock hit them. Eventually, they began to adjust to the change of environment and lifestyle. Three of my children have their own families now, and all of them are stable with their lives. I now have four grandchildren.

I am thankful for the SIV privilege that my father and I have received from the American government. It's not only a privilege but also a chance that we can give our family to have better opportunities.

A good future for my children was my dream. Sacrifice and determination helped me to make it happen.

Our two generations of SIV are great stories to tell my grandchildren. It is a unique story brought to us by this country we've served for a long time.

21

SONIA ROLLE

Administrative Management Assistant
U. S Commercial Service, Department of Commerce
20 years of service

You are given an option to try and a freedom to choose. Give yourself the courage to try. It may open a new opportunity, a whole new experience, and a new blessing. Sonia chose the option to try. It brought her closer to the love of her life.

W hen you live a comfortable life in the Philippines, with successful children, a job that you love, and surrounded with wonderful friends and relatives, you may think that living in America isn't for you.

Initially, my decision to immigrate in the "land of milk and honey" wasn't appealing. I had no reason to immigrate. The option to live with my daughter and her family in Canada was something I was considering. To be with my grandchildren was my priority.

After a thorough analysis of my life and retirement years, and with the encouragement of my former colleagues, I decided to avail myself of the SIV privilege. I'm so grateful that I did.

My grandchildren, Brice, Brie and Jonas are the love of my life. They bring me more smiles, laughter, and a bunch of happiness.

I immigrated in 2015 and stayed with my relative in Seattle, Washington. I purposely chose to settle in Washington so I could be closer to my grandchildren, Brice & Brie in Calgary, Canada.

The experience of living in America has changed my perspective. I now travel back and forth between these two countries.

I have the best of both worlds.

Being a "green card holder" is a great opportunity. It's a unique privilege we acquire from working for the American government. I wanted to experience being an immigrant in this country that I've served for 20 years. And I'm proud to be one.

I have a vast network of great friends and relatives in many parts of America. To visit them often is something I enjoy. It makes me feel at home.

I miss many things about living in the Philippines, such as the beauty of rural life and my previous job. I also miss my two other children and their families, especially my grandson, Jonas, my siblings, relatives, and great friends. The fun of hanging out with them and sharing laughter are precious moments to remember. I'm glad that modern technology connects me with them anytime I want.

I'm now retired and enjoying my life with many blessings.

To be closer to my two wonderful grandchildren in Canada is one of the best things that happened in my life. I want to hug them often and see them grow.

SIV is a great opportunity to welcome a new experience. If you have the same situation as me, I suggest you go for it. Enjoy a new experience and a new blessing.

22

DEOMIDES BLANDO

Education Liaison Representative
U.S. Department of Veterans Affairs
20 years of service

Resilience is the ability to overcome the unexpected. Humility is a virtue that occurs in the absence of pride. Gratefulness takes us to where we want to go. Deo was not only prepared but also packed his family's luggage with these secret ingredients to success. Plus, his humor and faith have been their guidance in this journey.

If you want to have a smooth transition from an established life in the Philippines to America, you need enough funds to support your lifestyle for at least a couple of years. If money is an issue, you must be resilient and practical.

Below is an account of how we started out in our journey here in America. Hopefully, recounting the timeline would give readers some idea when they decide to take the plunge.

Our family of three arrived in Orlando, Florida on February 1, 2019. We received our social security numbers two weeks after we arrived and permanent resident cards after three months. The first thing we purchased was a mobile phone family plan. This facilitated our communications to families and friends in America, who are our strong support system as we begin our lives as new immigrants.

As soon as we received our social security numbers, we opened our bank account. Thanks to our host in Jacksonville, Florida, the Ola family who offered to use their address, we could open a bank account.

We visited a family in Lincoln, Nebraska while waiting for our permanent resident cards. For us to move around, we began the process of acquiring a driver's license. The driver's license is probably the most important thing to secure, especially if you want to be independently mobile.

Social security numbers and proof of legal stay are required for the driver's license application. Two proofs of mailing address within the area of the Department of Motor Vehicles Office jurisdiction where we applied, was also required. To produce a proof of mailing address, my sister and brother-in-law purchased some items from Amazon on our behalf. The receipt was enough proof of a mailing address. We passed the online examination and actual driving test and got our driver's license.

We wanted to see some places of interest before we settled. We visited Virginia, the Washington D.C. area, Niagara Falls, New Jersey, and New York. This was also our reward for completing 20 years of employment and the tedious tasks in completing the SIV application.

In April 2019, we went back to Jacksonville, Florida. We were again fortunate and extremely thankful to be hosted by the Ola family. Major things on our to do list were accomplished. We changed our driver's license from Nebraska to Florida, opened an account with a credit union, purchased a brand-new car under bank financing, and secured a one-bedroom apartment. Acquiring the car and apartment was our biggest transitional move.

Some apartment offices require ample show money in the bank. Others require proof of adequate and regular income. And some only require a guarantor. We were fortunate that our host family agreed to be our guarantor. Hence, we moved into our apartment after about a week. The next two weeks were spent buying stuff for our new "home." My wife also got a job offer; thanks to a direct referral from our support group.

We didn't immediately enroll our son in the school we wanted him to go to, which was a mistake. We waited to visit the school after the kindergarten sections were filled up. Our recourse was to go to the office of the Duval County Public School to put him on the waiting list. We were asked to indicate a good reason why we wanted him enrolled in that school and to wait for status if they would accommodate my son. However, we couldn't wait for the decision, so we enrolled him in our next school of choice. Unfortunately, when the County Public School office contacted us that he was accepted to our initial school of choice, we had to decline.

We were required to submit the following documents to the school: my son's birth certificate, vaccination record from the public health office in Florida, and a medical certificate from a medical clinic.

To date, we are just on our first year as immigrants. I was recently hired as economic self-sufficiency specialist at the Department of Children and Families. As elsewhere, we have good and bad experiences; we have ups and downs. But we are truly grateful for family, friends, and former colleagues from Veterans Affairs who supported and coached us on our journey so far.

We have a long way to go. But we are confident that we can make it there successfully with our support system, our resilience, and our humility to acknowledge that we need guidance from those who "have been there" and those who "have done that."

Lastly, two things you need to bring with you (super abundantly) when you decide to make this trans-pacific journey: your limitless sense of humor and your endless faith in God.

23

ROSENDO PADUA

Visa Assistant
Immigrant Visa, Consular Office
20 years of service

We all have stories of heroic deeds or even a simple act of kindness. It doesn't matter how big or small your good deeds are, what matters is the difference you've made. Ross was given a challenging job. His dedication and courage have earned him admiration and gained him success.

My journey to SIV started from Russia. I was a young medical student in Moscow when I met my wife, who was a nurse. We got married and later had two daughters.

My study was put on hold, as I had to work for my family. The American Embassy in Moscow hired me in 1992 as a third country national with the position of a

controller/receptionist. I worked together with Americans, Australians, and Canadians.

A crisis happened in 1993. I experienced a dangerous and life-threatening situation in ensuring the safety of American diplomats during the time of crisis. That incident gave me a learning experience, and I earned trust from my supervisors. Eventually, they promoted me to a security investigator position.

More conflict happened because of interrogation and harassment of my position. With a strong sense of loyalty and commitment to my duties, I refused to cooperate. Subsequently, they ordered a deportation proceeding against me and my family. We left Russia in 2001 to go back to the Philippines.

I spent ten years at the American Embassy in Moscow. The constitutional crisis in Russia in 1993 has been a big part of my professional and personal growth. It has taught me values and a profound appreciation of life.

With my long and loyal service to the embassy in Moscow, the former U.S. Ambassador to Moscow, Alexander Vershbow gave me a recommendation to continue my service at the American Embassy in the Philippines.

In 2002, the American Embassy in the Philippines hired me as a visa clerk. I've learned a vast knowledge of immigration law, systems, and processes. I became a motivator, mentor, and leader. My fulfilled service lasted almost ten years.

My family and I immigrated to America in 2013. I wanted to fulfill a lifelong dream of giving my family a brighter future. We settled in Chicago, Illinois with a friend.

In the beginning, it was hard to find a job, given the experience I had. Later, I got a job as a customer service agent by a major airline at O'Hare International Airport. That job lasted for four years.

My current job is a security access controller, similar to my earlier experience in Russia. I enjoy what I do, and it allows me to use my customer service skills. I recently received an award from the company. This shows that when you love what you do, recognition isn't hard to attain.

Svetlana, my youngest daughter graduated with an accounting degree, and became a certified public accountant in the Philippines. Fortunately, she has a career that's in demand and it helped her find a job as soon as we arrived. While working full time, she got a student loan to study for a master's degree in accountancy. She's now married and recently became a certified public accountant in the U.S.

The older one, Genevieve graduated with a communications arts degree in the Philippines. She took computer courses to elevate her career. She was a scholar in DeVry University and attained her master's degree in computer networking and communications.

Our daughters finished their master's degree with distinction. They're on the right path to achieving their dreams and my dreams for them. We're proud parents.

My wife, Rebecca found a job as a caregiver after a few weeks of our arrival. Her nursing degree came in handy.

I miss my family and friends in the Philippines and the embassy work. But I'm living a new life in America to fulfill my "American dream."

There are many great things living here. Healthcare is one good thing that we enjoy. Saving money is easy to do if you're good with financial management. I have siblings in the Philippines, and I try to help them as much as I can. Studying is another good thing. Student loans are easily accessible if you know where to find them.

In every endeavor, there's a corresponding struggle. Everyone of us will go through challenges. Be ready to face them with strength and courage. This is the way to succeed.

My journey from Russia, to the Philippines, and finally to America, is worth every pain.

If there's no pain, there's no gain.

24

VIC CASTULO

Supply Technician
U. S. Department of Veterans Affairs
20 years of service

There's no easy roadmap to success. Right attitude is a tool to follow that roadmap. Trials and errors are learning curves. Vic has made a stop along the way, but he's enjoying the ride. He has the right tools and determined to achieve his goal and arrive at his destination.

I immigrated in August 2015 with my wife. We were sad to leave our three overaged children in the Philippines, but we needed to do it for them.

Having relatives to guide you in the early stage of transition is always beneficial. For this reason, we chose to settle on the beautiful island of O'ahu in Hawaii. I was fortunate to get a job immediately as a maintenance supervisor.

To live in Hawaii is like living in paradise with warm weather all year round. But all these are not free. The standard of living in Hawaii is high. Many residents have two or three jobs to keep up with expenses.

The best thing about living in Hawaii for me was the presence of Filipino culture. Anywhere you turn, you'll see Filipinos and hear Tagalog language. In our neighborhood, 80% of the population is Filipino. We buy, cook, and eat Filipino food every day. It seems like we didn't leave the Philippines.

The longer I stayed in Hawaii, the more I realized that owning a house there is difficult to achieve. It prompted me to explore another state.

A friend and a former colleague, Alex, encouraged me to move to Indiana where his family lives. I didn't give it a second thought and relocated in March 2017. I was hired at Purdue University as a custodian. Later, my wife got a job at the same university. We have a community of Filipinos working at Purdue University. Just as in the Philippines, we get together every weekend.

I didn't waste time in processing my children's immigration papers. I submitted the paperwork as soon as I arrived in Hawaii. I'm looking forward to the day they will finally arrive. In the meantime, we try to visit the Philippines when possible.

Since we moved to Indiana, our lifestyle has changed for the better. We have a simple life, good jobs, and are surrounded with friends. We plan to acquire our own house before our children arrive.

I'm grateful for the SIV opportunity. I experienced living in paradise for over a year and a half. Most importantly, my children will also experience living in America; that's my goal.

It's okay to make wrong choices or decisions sometimes. Use them as lessons learned. But don't stay where you are. Move on. Find the right place where life is easier and more promising.

25

JUDE LOPEZ

Administrative Clerk
Public Affairs Office
19 years and 6 months of service

Blessing comes not only in unexpected ways but also at unexpected times. When it does, use it to your advantage and be grateful. Jude didn't expect this wonderful blessing to come. His faith and prayers have brought him and his family to where they are.

I live in New York with my wife and three children ages 22, 16, and 7. We immigrated in June 2017. After a month, I got my first job as a dietary aid at a nursing home. I stayed in that job for two years until I was hired as a senior patient care assistant at Staten Island University Hospital Northwell Health. Many of us find it hard to get a job in the beginning because we don't have the local

experience. I'm thankful for a friend at church who introduced and recommended me for the job.

The Human Resources office at the hospital advised me to study medical technology that's useful in my career advancement. I was told that my degree in engineering would be accredited. I plan to pursue it soon.

My older son works as a pharmacy technician at a big pharmacy chain, CVS. He studied industrial pharmacy at the University of the Philippines but had to stop to keep his permanent resident status. My son has always been a scholar, and I'm a proud father. We don't want to waste his talents, and I support his plan to continue his studies. He's shifting career to information technology and just received a scholarship to begin next school year.

My daughter is another pride in the family. She's in tenth grade and is on the top list of the honor section. My wife works part time while she takes care of my younger son who's in second grade.

Our transition was less difficult because of family support. We currently live with my sister and her family. We hope to have a place of our own soon.

I have a blessed life in America with my family, a good job, and a brighter future for my children.

All this happened because of my employment at the American Embassy and the people who helped me. I am thankful for the SIV privilege. It's not just an opportunity but also an unexpected blessing.

Faith and prayer also make things possible.

26

CHRISTOPHER ALFONSO

Administrative Clerk
U.S. Commercial Service, Department of Commerce
18 years and 6 months of service

Adversity tests your character. It leads you to a great opportunity and blessings. Christopher has experienced some amount of adversity. He handled it well and has achieved the prize of his hardships.

Did you dream of working in the Pentagon? I immigrated to America and didn't expect to work at the headquarters of the Department of Defense - the Pentagon.

Here's my story:

Our office in Manila had a reorganization. Sometime in October 2016, my boss called me into her office to tell me the unexpected news that my position would be abolished.

Consequently, I would be affected by the reduction-in-force.

I was surprised and sad. I told my family and relocated them back to my hometown, while I was trying to figure out what was going to happen after losing my job. Our relocation resulted in my commuting to work of two hours (one way) for six months. It was hard, but I needed to do it. I was thinking of our future, and was worried that I couldn't avail myself of the SIV opportunity, since I hadn't completed my 20 years of service.

The human resources office informed me that I could apply for SIV because they're eliminating my position. I got excited and started to prepare the documents I needed. It gave me hope.

I submitted my SIV package, feeling positive. Meanwhile, I was waiting for the last date of my employment, which lasted for a few more months.

Almost the same time the office told me of my termination date, I also received great news: my SIV application was approved. I had tears of joy.

My journey continues.

I left the Philippines by myself in March 2017 and stayed with my relatives in Virginia. I decided to leave my family behind to have a faster transition.

One day, while I was dining at 1521 Bistro Filipino Restaurant with my relatives, I learned that the restaurant was hiring. I was eager to start working, so I went back the following day to apply. I was hired as a food runner, then after three weeks, I was promoted to a line cook.

I found a part-time job at Westin Hotel doing room service. Eventually, I resigned at Bistro Filipino, as I couldn't keep both jobs with the same schedule.

A former friend at the Bistro told me about a job opening at the Market Basket, a popular catering company that has a location in the Pentagon. I applied and was hired. The hiring process took about two weeks to finish. They gave me a three-day training, then I was initially assigned to work at the American section.

I am now an assistant chef in the Pentagon.

My first day at work brought back memories of the American Embassy in Manila. The security procedure wasn't new to me. It was similar but more high profile. I was excited and nervous.

I was finally settled jobwise, so it was time for my family to come. My oldest daughter arrived in March of 2018. She also got her first job at the Bistro Filipino as a hostess. Now she works as a manager at McDonald's. My wife and my two younger daughters followed.

The SIV was an unexpected blessing that my family has received. I feel fortunate and thankful.

Honesty and good relationship at work will help build your integrity. They are your foundation to obtain the SIV privilege.

Good planning, hard work, and determination are tools you can use to settle in and achieve things that may be beyond your expectations.

EPILOGUE

Being a flight attendant is in my blood. I loved giving our customers the best experience I can. Everyone boards the plane with baggage and I'm not talking about the physical kind. They all have worries, stresses, and anticipation with them as they board. So, although I have to leave my baggage at the door, which is often not an easy task, I love helping make our passengers' day a bit lighter for them. And sometimes I've had the privilege of making their day a lot better. Whether it's moving someone's seat for them or helping someone who is fearful and needs a hand to hold, or listening to their happy or sad story, it's truly what I was put on this earth to do along with writing. Please see an article about one of my many missions to help passengers on page 101.

Jonathan, my eldest, finished with a computer engineering degree from the top engineering school in the Philippines. After graduation he went to work for the U.S. based company Oracle for the next four years. Although this kept him in the Philippines longer, it provided him with the necessary experience to ease his transition to America. He now works as a consultant for a government agency in Maryland. His

wife and children are still overseas but we expect them to join all of us soon. And I can't wait, because I promised both my grandkids a trip to Disney when they get here.

My daughter, Mary Frances, finished her accounting degree and became a certified public accountant. She is now living in New York City working for a large accounting firm, Ernst and Young. She has inherited my passion for travel.

In 2018, my youngest son, Joshua, arrived in the United States and finished his final year of high school. My heart warmed with pride when we found out he got accepted to Information Technology High School in New York. He pushed himself to do well in school. He also worked part-time as a way to gain some friends and acclimate to the culture as I had years earlier. Later in his senior year, Joshua received a scholarship from the City University of New York to study computer science. Whatever Joshua decides to do with his future, I know he will be amazing.

My eyes fill with tears of joy and my heart is full as I finish this book. I hope I have given you a glimpse into what it is like to immigrate to America. The road is not easy. It's filled with disappointment, sacrifice, and hard work. Have faith in yourself, in your family, and rely on any means to gain knowledge and experience. The process is long but worth it in the end, at least it was for me and for the 25 others who generously shared their stories.

NOTEWORTHYNEWS

Flight Attendant Helps Distressed Mother Reunite with Son at JFK

Our Flight Attendants are trained to keep a high level of situational awareness at all times.

Recently, while performing her preflight duties from Bangor, Maine, to LGA, Lia Ocampo saw a customer who appeared anxious and emotional. Once everyone had taken their seats, Lia approached the customer, who introduced herself as Nancy.

Nancy was busy trying to organize documents, respond to emails and texts on her phone, and needed more room than her current seat assignment afforded her. Extending an empathetic hand, Lia offered to move Nancy to an empty row and even helped carry her briefcase to the new seat. Little did Lia know that this simple gesture would turn into an adventure leading to an emotional reunion.

Nancy's son, Derek, had spent the past year in South Korea serving as an English teacher to school-aged children. Derek's employment at the school had come to an end, and his family elected to help him move back home—halfway around the world—to Portland.

The long journey was overwhelming for Derek and further exacerbated a health issue, so he boarded his flight to New York City without a cell phone or any way to contact his family.

Upon landing at JFK, the process of transitioning through customs caused Derek to become disoriented, losing track of time and missing his connection. He spent the night in the airport and missed his early morning flight, which raised alarms with Nancy.

Fearing her son had gone missing, Nancy bought a last-minute ticket to LGA. Her plan was to grab a cab to JFK in the hopes she might find him waiting in the arrivals area, all the while fighting off the "what if's" of person alone in the largest metropolis in the United States.

Lia's flight to LGA was the last of a long trip. She was eager to get on her commuting flight home to Florida, but having heard Nancy's predicament, she opted to stay with her customer and ensure she was able to find her son. At the very least, she wanted to help Nancy get to JFK and start the process.

As Lia led Nancy on to a shuttle bus between terminals, Nancy's phone rang. It was Derek's sister, who had been contacted by a Delta gate agent. Derek was safe — tired and nervous, but safe — and had been rebooked on the last flight that night. Nancy and Lia hugged, a few tears were shed, and a smile that had been strained by the stress of the unknown returned to Nancy's face.

"While en route to JFK, Nancy worked with Delta to change her return flight back to Portland to leave that night from JFK with Derek," said Lia. "I accompanied her through security at Terminal 4, and the search to find Derek was on."

The two hustled through T4 with purpose, checking every gate area and bench for Derek. Lia and Nancy then took the jitney bus from B55 to Terminal 2 to search the gate area his flight was scheduled out of that night.

As they stepped off the bus, Nancy's phone rang again — it was her daughter, informing her that Derek was now at B55. So, the dash continued with a hop back onto the jitney. Lia stayed by Nancy's side the entire time, holding her hand and ensuring she knew where she needed to go.

"Once we got back to T4, there he was," Lia noted. "Nancy was so relieved and happy to see her son. They hugged. I saw the emotions pour out from both of them. I was happy to have helped guide Nancy through this difficult journey, and Derek assured her that he wouldn't miss the flight again."

Thank you, Lia, for your exceptional dedication to this mother in her time of need. Your empathy and compassion elevate beyond the normal call of duty. ✈

What I Know For Sure
A Compilation of Wisdom

- ❖ Celebrate your big and small accomplishments. It's a way to enjoy life and achieve more goals.

- ❖ If one plan doesn't work out, try to explore other options.

- ❖ Be prepared and confident. That's how to ace a job interview.

- ❖ Be resourceful and build contacts.

- ❖ Acquiring new training or education will upgrade your qualifications. It will help you relaunch your previous career or start a new one.

- ❖ Don't hesitate to ask for help. Be humble and thankful.

- ❖ Opportunities are around you. Be patient and have faith.

- ❖ Find a job where you'll have growth and happiness.

- ❖ Never give up on your dreams and don't be afraid to try.

- ❖ Find your passion.

- ❖ Don't let failure intimidate you, learn from it.

- ❖ Find your inspiration or create your own. Motivation creates accomplishments.

- ❖ Know your mission. And when you find your mission, grow with it.

- ❖ Always look for an opportunity to do good deeds. It creates blessings.

- ❖ Create your vision board to achieve your goals. Learn the power of writing your goals down.

- ❖ Always remember those people who helped you along the way, especially those who were with you through tough times.

- ❖ When you help someone succeed, you will become successful.

- ❖ It doesn't matter if the journey is short or long. What matters is the process of learning and sharing your wisdom with others.

- ❖ Gratefulness is the key to more blessings and happiness. Be thankful. Share your blessings.

I hope ***What We Know For Sure*** helps you move faster toward your desired destination and closer to your best self.

ACKNOWLEDGMENTS

I created this book out of a strong desire to help others. I put it on my vision board along with the rest of my goals and eventually the right timing and concept came to me. After five years that vision is now a reality.

To my children Jonathan, Mary Frances, and Joshua, thank you for your unconditional love and generous hearts. You make me proud. To my family in the Philippines, my sister Liz, and brother Zeus, for being my prayer warriors and providing me with moral support because you knew you couldn't stop me from doing what I want to do. To my Aunt Paz who provided me with financial support while I was studying.

With gratitude to my storytellers, for allowing and trusting me to share your stories. You didn't hesitate to say yes when I told you about the book project. Thank you for sharing your wisdom and helping me fulfill my "Mission Philippines." I am proud of what you've achieved, and I admire your sacrifices and struggles. Without your stories this book wouldn't have become a reality.

With gratitude to Ambassador Harry K. Thomas, Jr., for taking part in this book. The honor is all mine. You're a boss, mentor, and friend to us. We've shared many great and memorable experiences during your time at the embassy. You presented us with numerous awards and approved most of our Special Immigrant Visas. Thank you for knowing us in many aspects of our lives and for your admiration.

With gratitude to Thess Sula, for being a friend and mentor. And for your invaluable support and encouragement. There's no other person who could write the foreword of my first book better than you.

To Ning Ning Mercado, for being my friend and adopted sister. For your support in everything including my goal to write this book and your expertise in providing me with guidance. To my former colleagues and friends from the American Embassy, thank you for the camaraderie and the professional relationship we've built together. I am looking forward to writing some of your stories in the next volume of this book. To my former bosses at the embassy, thank you for your trust and guidance to help me perform my job well. Thank you for the awards and recommendations that got me the Special Immigrant Visa.

To Endeavor Air, for giving me my dream job. To the management in JFK Airport, particularly Eugene Joaquin who has been my mentor and manager. To my former recruitment and mentoring teams, who gave me the experience to share my skills. To my travel buddy, John Culala, for our many travel adventures we've been on together. I am looking forward to exploring more wonders of the world with you.

To my flight attendant and pilot colleagues, friends, and adopted kids in the aviation world who share with me the passion of what we do. To our customers on my flights who appreciated what I did for them and had fun with me while I did my job. The wonderful people and great experiences I encounter on every single flight gives me more reasons to love what I do.

To my adopted aunt, Tita Siony, who was my company for a few months when I was starting my life in New York, and for being my prayer warrior. To my friends in the Philippines, in the United States and other parts of the world. I can't name all of you but thank you for all the support and encouragement. To my college "Advocate" team where I started to prove that I love to write. Thanks for the longtime friendship we've built. To the CNN iReport team. Thank you for the "CNN iReport Spirit" award that proved my love for storytelling and photography. To my CNN iReport friends who shared with me the passion of iReporting and volunteer work.

To Thembie Sibanda, who welcomed me during my trip to Victoria Falls, Zimbabwe. You didn't know me, but you helped me in fulfilling my "Mission Africa." To my adopted girls in Africa, thank you for letting me share with you a part of who I am.

To my technical team: Celeste Chin from Creative License Publishing for editorial work and advice. Wayne Purdin from Upwork for editorial work. Digital Publishing of Florida, Ryan and Jill Illg for book design and printing. Aubrey Millan for the book cover design, and advice. And to my Marketing Consultant, Angelica Cabahug. Thank you all for your patience and sharing your expertise with me.

My profound gratitude to my sounding board, John, thank you for everything.

Special mention to my favorite authors, Oprah, Og Mandino, and Wayne Dyer. The wisdom I've learned from you has been my guide and ultimately motivated me to write this book.

I am forever grateful to those who guided and helped me to my successful SIV transition from the Philippines to America. To those who have been a part of my life for a season and a reason, thank you.

I am fortunate to have all of you on this rewarding journey. I couldn't have done this without you. Thank you.

Until the next journey.

ABOUT THE AUTHOR

Lia Ocampo is a multifaceted individual with a passion for writing, reading, and helping others. She credits her beloved mother for raising her with a deep love of education, a strong value system, and a solid work ethic. It was during her formative years when Lia's mom shared with her a book called "University of Success" by Og Mandino. This book became Lia's inspiration to pursue excellence in everything she does.

After receiving a bachelor's degree in English from the University of Batangas, Lia headed to Manila to start her career. She began her career with the U.S. Refugee Program which lasted four years. From there, Lia spent the next 18 years working for the American Embassy in the following Departments: Human Resources office of the U.S. Department of State, U.S. Trade and Development Agency, Public Affairs Office, and U.S. Department of Veterans Affairs.

While working at the embassy, Lia fostered her love for writing. She became a freelance writer for an online news company, Allvoices, eventually winning the "Most Viewed Asia Pacific News" award in 2010. Her passion for social justice also took form at this time. Lia joined World Pulse, a social networking community aimed at connecting women to inspire change in the world. Motivated to share her many experiences and wisdom, Lia wrote blogs, one of them is called *What Lia Knows for Sure*.

In 2012, Lia immigrated to the United States where she continued on her writing for CNN iReport as a citizen journalist. She's writing stories about people and the good deeds they performed. She had more than 140 stories vetted by CNN, some of which were featured online or on television. Lia was also the recipient of the "CNN iReport Spirit Award" in 2013. Just one year later, Lia continued to strive for success in her professional life as she achieved her lifelong goal of becoming a flight attendant–a career she holds and loves to this day.

On her 50th birthday, while others might be celebrating their accomplishments, Lia continued to push herself to do more. She challenged herself to complete 50 hours of volunteer work, finish exploring 50 lighthouses, and travel to 50 countries. As if these lofty goals weren't enough, she created what she called "Mission Africa." This mission was designed to unofficially adopt five teenage girls from Zimbabwe and teach them how to set and achieve their goals. She not only fulfilled this personal mission but was inspired to create "Mission Philippines." The purpose of "Mission Philippines" was to collect and share stories of former embassy colleagues to spread their collective wisdom to others which eventually was the impetus for her first book, *What We Know for Sure*.

Lia currently resides in Florida and New York, where she remains dedicated to her writing and her love of travel and people. Look for her next book about her love for traveling and more inspirational stories.